BOARDING SCHOOLS AND THE INDIGENOUS STORY

OTHER BOOKS IN THE RACE TO THE TRUTH SERIES

Colonization and the Wampanoag Story

Slavery and the African American Story

Exclusion and the Chinese American Story

Borderlands and the Mexican American Story

Abolition and the African American Story

BOARDING SCHOOLS AND THE INDIGENOUS STORY

RACE TO THE TRUTH

Ashley Fairbanks

CROWN BOOKS FOR YOUNG READERS
NEW YORK

Crown Books for Young Readers
An imprint of Random House Children's Books
A division of Penguin Random House LLC
1745 Broadway, New York, NY 10019
penguinrandomhouse.com
rhcbooks.com

For interior image credits, see page 216.

Editor: Kelly Delaney
Cover Designer: Jade Rector
Interior Designer: Jen Valero
Production Editors: Patricia Callahan and Jamie Johnson
Managing Editor: Tisha Paul
Production Manager: Tim Terhune

Library of Congress Cataloging-in-Publication Data is available upon request.
ISBN 978-0-593-81139-9 (trade) — ISBN 978-0-593-81140-5 (lib. bdg.) — ISBN 978-0-593-81141-2 (ebook)

The text of this book is set in 12.5-point Adobe Garamond Pro.

Printed in the United States of America
1st Printing

The authorized representative in the EU for product safety and compliance is Penguin Random House Ireland, Morrison Chambers, 32 Nassau Street, Dublin D02 YH68, Ireland, https://eu-contact.penguin.ie.

For my gramma emma and all of the survivors

CONTENTS

LITTLE BEAR'S LONG JOURNEY

Not so long ago, in the year 1900, in the vast plains of America, there lived a young American Indian child named Mato Cikala, or Little Bear. Little Bear belonged to the Lakota people. He lived happily with his mother, father, and three younger sisters in a small but cozy tipi by a large lake. Little Bear loved to listen to the stories told by his elders around the campfire and run freely across the grassy prairie with his friends.

One day, when the sun was high in the sky and the birds were singing, strangers came to their village. These strangers were dressed differently. The sweat on their foreheads shimmered like water under the sun. They had serious faces and carried papers in their hands. Little Bear watched with curiosity as the strangers talked with the elders.

After a while, the strangers turned to Little Bear's family. They spoke in a language he didn't understand, but their tone was serious. Little Bear's parents looked worried. He felt a knot forming in his stomach, sensing that something was very wrong.

The strangers gestured toward Little Bear, and his parents nodded sadly. He didn't know what was happening, but he could see the tears in his parents' eyes. Before Little Bear could comprehend what was going on, the strangers took his hand and led him away from the only home he had ever known.

As they walked, Little Bear looked back at his family, watching them grow smaller and smaller in the distance. He could hear his father crying. Fear gripped his heart as he wondered where he was being taken and why he couldn't stay with his family. He loved his life, catching fish, playing with his cousins. He knew children who had gone with the white men before, and he had never seen them again.

After a long journey, Little Bear arrived at a place unlike anything he had ever seen before. It was a large building made of brick and surrounded by high fences. He felt a pang of fear as he realized that this was to be his new home. The strangers tried to explain where they were, but Little Bear couldn't understand.

Little Bear felt lost and alone in this unfamiliar place. Everything seemed so strange and different, from the language spoken to the clothes worn by the other children and adults. He missed his family terribly and longed to be back in the comfort of their tipi.

When he awoke the next day, Little Bear was given a set of new clothes and uncomfortable shoes. A white woman inspected him from head to toe and forced him to sit still as she cut his long hair far above his ears. He was embarrassed, as men in his community cut their hair only when they were grieving. He looked in the mirror and could barely recognize himself. They began to call him a white man's name, Thomas. He hated it.

At this strange place, Native children, only some of whom were Lakota like him, were taught English, mathematics, and other subjects that were foreign to Little Bear. They had been forced to abandon their languages, customs, and traditions in favor of these new ways. Little Bear struggled to adapt to this way of life. He felt like a fish out of water.

Despite longing for home, Little Bear found happiness in the friendships he formed with other children at the school. Together, they whispered in their Native languages, teaching each other words they were forbidden to say during the day. The children who spoke his language told him they were at a place called Flandreau Indian School. Some of them had been here for years without leaving. Amid their sadness, they found joy in stories and memories of life at home.

But as the days turned into weeks and the weeks turned into months, Little Bear couldn't shake the feeling of homesickness that gnawed at his heart. He missed the sound of his mother laughing, the familiar words of his language, the smell of the grass after a summer rain, and the warmth of his grandmother's embrace.

One night, as he lay in bed staring up at the ceiling, a wave of determination washed over him. He knew that he couldn't stay at this Indian school forever, far away from everything he held dear. He had to find a way back to his family, back to where he belonged.

The next day, Little Bear approached one of the teachers at the school and shared his desire to return home. The teacher was impatient with him and explained that leaving the school was not an option. Little Bear felt a surge of frustration and despair, but deep down, he refused to give up hope.

Months passed, and Little Bear began to dream of escape. He spent his days observing the routines of the school, looking for any opportunity to slip away unnoticed. And then, one day, his chance came.

During a fire drill, things grew chaotic as teachers and students rushed to evacuate the building. In the confusion, Little Bear broke away from the crowd and darted toward the school gates. With his heart pounding and his hands trembling, he pushed open the heavy doors and ran as fast as his legs could carry him.

Through the fields and prairies, across rivers and valleys, Little Bear ran, driven by the longing to be reunited with his family. He followed the railroad tracks for as long as he could. Along the way, he faced challenges, such as hunger and exhaustion. He was so afraid of being caught and returned to the school. But through it all, he never lost sight of his goal.

Finally, after what felt like an eternity, Little Bear reached the familiar plains of his homeland. He found the local mission school, where some of his cousins attended, and they ran home to their village together. Tears of joy streamed down his face as he ran toward his family's home, his heart bursting with love and relief.

When he arrived, his parents greeted him with open arms and tears of happiness. His family had never stopped hoping and praying for his safe return, and now their prayers had been answered. It felt so good to hear his real name from his mother's lips again—Mato Cikala, not Thomas. As he sat around the campfire that night, surrounded by loved ones and bathed in the warm glow of the flames, he felt a sense of calm wash over him.

And as he drifted off to sleep, he whispered a silent promise to himself—no matter where life took them, he would always find his way home.

INTRODUCTION

The story of Little Bear is a work of fiction, but it is similar to the stories of hundreds of thousands of Indigenous children who were taken away from their homes during the nineteenth and twentieth centuries. Children like Little Bear were taken away to boarding schools run by the United States government. Boarding schools were just one chapter in the mistreatment of Indigenous people on this continent since European colonization began in earnest in 1492. Throughout this book, we will use stories like this to help you put yourself in the shoes of children who experienced impossibly hard things. The stories of Little Bear, Ahyoka, Lila, James and Auntie Bineshi, and Ode are all fiction, but represent very real experiences.

Think about your home—your bedroom, your favorite things, your family and loved ones. For most people, home is a place that feels safe and makes us comfortable. We are used to the food, the sounds, and the language that is spoken around us. For children especially, home and the communities we live in are really all we know.

But for many Native American children in recent history, the comfort of home was stolen away from them by actions of religious institutions and European colonizers. Why did this happen? Because European settlers wanted to destroy Indigenous ways of life, get tribes to convert to their religions and assimilate into their cultures, or make them disappear entirely.

Starting in the 1860s and continuing until the 1940s, hundreds of thousands of Native American children from tribes across the country, some as young as five, were taken from their families and sent to one of the at least 526 boarding schools run by the U.S. government or churches.

Often against their parents' will, the children were taken to schools that were completely unfamiliar to them. Indigenous children were removed from the world they knew. They were forced to dress in new clothes, their own clothes and belongings taken from them. They were often forced to cut their hair, something that was deeply traumatizing for children whose cultures see hair as something sacred. Many tribes believe hair is to be cut only when mourning or suffering great loss.

A portrait of Tom Torlino, a Navajo, wearing his native clothing in 1882.

Tom Torlino in 1885, in his Carlisle Indian School uniform and haircut.

These boarding schools could be days' or weeks' travel from the reservations where the children were born. For many students, this could mean that they weren't able to see their friends, families, or homes for months, even years, at a time. In the summer, rather than getting a vacation like kids today, some boarding school students were hired out for farm labor or domestic service (like cooking or cleaning) for white families in neighboring communities.

At the National Archives, where the government keeps the records for all their agencies, you can find the records of the government boarding schools. In letters, parents often request for their children to come home to participate in ceremonies, to visit with sick relatives, or simply because they are missed by their family. Reply letters from schools often deny these requests.

For decades, survivors of the boarding schools, both the government-created and church-run schools, have told their stories. They recount how they weren't allowed to speak their Indigenous languages or keep in contact with their families. Many survivors talk about how they were mistreated and subject to verbal, physical, and sexual abuse.

Because they spent so long away from home, Native American boarding school students often returned home to communities that were now unfamiliar. Many had lost the ability to speak their Indigenous language, so it was hard to communicate with the friends and loved ones they'd been forced to leave behind. Students who had been taken from their communities had missed learning critical skills needed to survive in a traditional way. The theft of their Indigenous language meant they didn't have access to important cultural traditions. All of this made many boarding school survivors feel like they no longer belonged with their people.

The boarding school system didn't just harm the

Indigenous children who were forced into it but left a lasting impact on generations of Indigenous families and communities. Because children had been removed from their parents and raised in harsh environments, they often didn't learn how to properly parent their own children when they grew up. The trauma of the boarding school experience could also create mental health issues that people didn't know how to cope with in healthy ways.

As Ojibwe historian Dr. Brenda Child once explained, these boarding schools are "our best monument to the history of colonial cruelty and dispossession, but one with the power to educate us about Indian survival, both past and present." Boarding school stories, like the ones contained here, aren't only stories of pain but stories of resilience—how strong Indigenous people have always been and remain today.

But why were the boarding schools started in the first place? Zitkála-Šá, a Dakota writer and activist who attended Carlisle Indian Industrial School, once wrote that boarding schools weren't founded with the mission of educating children; they were made to protect the power of white settlers and promote Christianity.

Boarding schools were only an extension of the violence of European colonizers, part of the cultural genocide of Indigenous people that had been taking place since Columbus arrived in 1492. White settlers wanted not only to take the land and resources of Indigenous people but also to get rid of their cultures altogether.

In this book, you'll learn the history of how European colonizers and eventually the U.S. government took the land of Indigenous people. You'll learn why boarding schools for Indigenous children came to exist, what life was like for students at these schools, and the legacy they left behind. You'll also learn some of the stories of students in the schools, and how their experience impacted their lives.

But you'll also learn that the U.S. government's efforts to remove Indigenous children from their families didn't end with boarding schools. For decades after most schools had closed, the government continued to put Indigenous children in foster care, adopt them out into white families, and separate them from their cultures. Indigenous children today are still removed from their families at the highest rates of any group.

Normally, when we talk about the history of Indigenous people, it's best to be specific about what tribe experienced something. But because boarding schools impacted children from so many tribes, we'll cover bits of history from across the continent.

American Indian vs. Native American vs. Indigenous

Throughout American history, people have used a lot of different names for the people who lived on this continent before Europeans arrived. For a long time, people called Indigenous Americans "Indians" because Christopher Columbus, upon arriving in a place he called "Hispaniola" and the Indigenous Taíno called "Quisqueya" (now Haiti and the Dominican Republic), believed he'd arrived in India. During the civil rights movement, "American Indian" was more popular, and later, "Native American" became the preference of some people.

Many people today prefer to say "Indigenous," as it affirms the status of American Indian people as the original inhabitants of this continent. Indigenous people across America have different preferences for what term they want to be called, and many prefer people to use their specific tribal name (like Lakota or Tongva or Diné). The best way to know what people prefer is just to ask.

In this book, we will use tribal names when speaking about specific people or tribes, and usually "Indigenous" to talk about all people originally living in the Americas and what would eventually become the United States.

WHAT ARE TRIBES?

Tribes are groups of Indigenous people. In the United States, 574 tribes are recognized by the federal government. The process of getting recognized can be difficult, so some tribes are recognized by state or even local governments. Federally recognized tribes and their citizens benefit from rights secured in treaties between the tribe and the federal government. The relationship between these tribes and the government is managed by an organization called the Bureau of Indian Affairs (BIA).

Every tribe has their own government services, like schools, businesses, and hospitals, depending on their size. There are very large tribes, with tens of thousands of citizens, and small tribes, with just a few dozen. Many tribes have a reservation, or a base of land where their tribe is headquartered and tribal members may live. Some reservations are bigger than small states. In addition to having their own governments, land bases, and citizens, tribes have their own languages, traditions, clothing, and religions. Citizens of different tribes were treated different ways by the government historically and have different experiences today. It's important to not generalize the histories, opinions, traditions, or values of different tribes, or of all Indigenous people, because we're all different!

CHAPTER 1

LIFE BEFORE COLONIZATION

Up until very recently, and still today in some places, students have been taught that Christopher Columbus, an explorer from Italy, "discovered" America. This is not true. While Columbus was the first European to arrive in the Caribbean, Indigenous people had already been here since time immemorial, or before anyone remembers. According to the creation stories of many Indigenous people, from Alaska to Chile, they have always been here. At places like Cactus Hill in Virginia or Huaca Prieta in Peru, there is evidence of settlement that goes back fifteen thousand to twenty thousand years. Indigenous people have been in the Americas for a very, very long time.

Still, despite the evidence, and the vibrant and

rich oral histories from many tribes, a lot of people don't really think about the story of America as starting before Columbus. This isn't an accident. It can be hard to accept the scale of the destruction during the initial colonization of the Americas, so many of us are never taught the real history of what happened to Indigenous people.

Prior to the arrival of European colonizers, America wasn't just an empty land waiting to be stumbled upon. The land we now know as the United States was inhabited by hundreds of tribes of Indigenous peoples. These distinct tribes and nations boasted a diverse array of cultures, languages, traditions, and ways of life.

It would take a lot of paper to tell you what all their lives were like before colonization began. So, in this chapter, I'll briefly tell you about some of the shared culture, values, and history of many Indigenous people. But as you read, it's important to remember that all tribes are different.

While this is a chapter about life before colonization, much of it is still true today. Many very, very terrible things have been done to Indigenous people, but we have survived. While we have faced unimaginable losses, our cultures, languages, and the ways that we see the world persist.

We are still here.

IT STARTS WITH THE LAND

Almost all Indigenous cultures, both long ago and today, have a strong connection to our homelands—the lands that we come from and have lived on. From generation to generation, Indigenous elders have passed on important knowledge of the world around us, knowledge that has been shaped by generations of living on the land and interacting with the animals that live on it as well. Indigenous people across the continent skillfully utilized the resources offered by their different environments for food, shelter, tools, and clothing.

Tribes relied on hunting, trapping, and fishing, and used various techniques to harvest an assortment of fruits, nuts, and plants. Many tribes also migrated seasonally, following animals and food where they were abundant at different times of year. Their deep understanding of the land and its offerings, combined with worldviews that often promoted respect of the interconnectedness of all creatures, allowed tribes to thrive. Indigenous people in the Americas were able to maintain a sustainable way of life for tens of thousands of years before Europeans arrived.

Many tribes across the Americas practiced agriculture, growing crops such as local varieties of corn, beans, and squash. For the tribes that farmed, growing food was vital to their survival and allowed for the development of more-permanent settlements. While many of these agricultural practices were nearly lost in the face of land theft, displacement, and genocide, there are growing efforts to restore Indigenous food systems today.

A profound respect for the land and nature and the connections between living things is built into the languages and cultures of many Indigenous peoples. Elders pass on an understanding of the delicate balance of ecosystems, the value of sustainable methods of resource management, and the belief that they are stewards of the land, responsible for its care and preservation for future generations. The connection between Indigenous people and the land is not like a fairy tale but a reality that is shaped by our cultural teachings.

What Is Genocide?

Genocide is a horrifying, tragic thing that one group of people can do to another. It means that a group of people tries to harm or completely kill off another group just because of their race, religion, or something else that makes them who they are. Or maybe because one group wants the resources and land of another.

The United Nations, which is a big group of countries that work together for peace and to help make the world a better place, has a definition of genocide. They say it is when acts are done to "destroy, in whole or part, a national, ethnical, racial, or religious group." This could be by killing people in the group, causing them serious harm, making it so hard for them to live that they would eventually be gone, stopping babies from being born within the group, or taking the children away from the group so they can't grow up with their families' culture and traditions.

COMMUNITY AND SOCIAL STRUCTURE

Indigenous people have always relied on strong bonds and interdependence (the idea that we all need each other) to meet our needs, ensuring not only survival but also the preservation of cultural traditions and values passed down over generations. Through collective efforts, Indigenous people navigated the challenges of their environments.

Many Indigenous societies have always been organized intricately around kinship relationships and clan systems. That means that the idea of family is usually much bigger than just parents and children, or even aunts, uncles, cousins, and grandparents. Families could extend to include people with shared connections, like clans—a grouping of people based on factors like geography or roles in society.

Depending on the tribe, children might inherit their clans from their mother, their father, or both. These clans can help people understand what their connection to other people in their tribe is, even if they are just meeting for the first time.

Most tribes taught immense respect for elders, seeing them as the most valuable members of the community because of the wealth of knowledge they'd built over a lifetime. Elders, both in the past and today, are the heart of Indigenous communities, playing an important role in raising and teaching children, and providing guidance and leadership for their people.

Just like elders, children were valued for the role

they played in their communities. They were seen as a tribe's most valuable resource, the entire future of their people. Because of this, the responsibility for raising a child wasn't placed just on their parents but on their entire family and clan, or even the entire tribe. Children were included in all activities, rather than being isolated in school all day.

Understanding how important family and roles in community can be to Indigenous peoples is important to understanding why the idea of taking children away from home and placing them in boarding schools had a devastating impact on not just the children but entire tribal communities.

What Is Resilience?

Imagine you're playing a game, and sometimes in the game, things don't go the way you want them to. Maybe you lose a round or your character gets knocked down. Resilience helps you bounce back when things don't go your way.

Resilience isn't about never feeling upset or facing challenges; it's about being able to handle those tough moments and keep moving forward. It's like having a superpower that helps you stay strong even when things get hard.

When we talk about the resilience of Indigenous people, it's a way of talking about their ability to stay strong even in the face of tremendous challenges. This doesn't mean that they don't feel the pain of bad things that have happened to them, but that they are able to keep going despite the hurt and loss they've experienced.

LEADERSHIP AND COUNCILS

Each tribe had its own unique form of governance that reflected their cultural values and traditions. Some tribes appointed chiefs, or leaders, who possessed exceptional wisdom and leadership qualities, guiding their communities with expertise and insight. These individuals were entrusted with making crucial decisions that shaped the destiny of their people.

In some communities, leaders may have been

chosen based on their clan, with one clan taking on the responsibility of leadership and upholding respect for the other clans, realizing that everyone has an important role to play in the society.

Other tribes relied on councils consisting of elders, whose accumulated knowledge and experience ensured the well-being of the community. These respected council members deliberated together to reach consensus and make important decisions that impacted the lives of their fellow tribe members.

TRADE AND INTERACTION

Indigenous peoples were not isolated from one another. Most tribes engaged in trade and interaction with both neighboring tribes and those that were very far away. Trade networks across the continent allowed for the exchange of goods, foods, and even cultural practices and religion.

Trade was an essential part of life for the Indigenous peoples of the Americas. These networks weren't just about trading items—they were also an important space for social interaction and diplomacy between tribes.

Trade items included things like seeds, shells, tools, and crafted goods. For instance, tribes in the coastal regions might trade shells and fish for corn and pottery from inland tribes. In the Great Plains, tribes hunted buffalo and could trade hides and meat for crops grown by farming tribes. This diversity in trade goods reflects the diverse ecosystems and lifestyles of Indigenous tribes.

In precontact times, before European colonizers arrived on their land, tribes didn't have wagons or pack animals like donkeys, so most trade happened in canoes, which were paddled down coastlines and through the large network of waterways and rivers that crisscross the American continent.

These trade networks also played a critical role in spreading technology, knowledge, and cultural practices. The spread of the bow-and-arrow technology is one such example—it started in one area and spread across the continent through trade networks. Similarly, ideas about philosophy, art, and social organization could spread and influence many tribes, contributing to the diversity of Indigenous cultures.

ART AND CULTURE

Indigenous cultures, deeply rooted in history and tradition, are and have always been rich with art and

A doll made by a fourth-grade class at Fort Defiance Boarding School in Arizona, 1945.

creativity. Through intricate quillwork (using porcupine quills to adorn objects), pottery, paintings, music, and dance, Indigenous people, both before colonization and today, express our stories, traditions, and values through art.

These diverse art forms not only reflect Indigenous ways of life but also serve as a powerful medium of communication, passing on knowledge and wisdom across time and place. Artwork doesn't just serve a purpose of making things beautiful; it could be used to mark ownership of objects, record the conditions, mark the passage of time, record historical events, or even give warnings about threats to a community.

Craftsmanship of objects like tipis, woven goods like rugs and blankets, basketry, and pottery also served a practical purpose, creating objects needed for survival or used for trade.

ORAL TRADITIONS AND TEACHING

While the cultures of the colonizers relied on the written word to pass on stories and to educate their people, Indigenous people in the Americas relied primarily on oral traditions, or knowledge that is passed on from one person to another. Oral traditions and storytelling are still very important to many Indigenous people today.

While Indigenous people didn't have formal schools, they taught their children how to survive through hands-on learning and taught them their history, values, and legends through stories passed down from generation to generation.

This dependence on oral tradition and intergenerational teaching meant that later, when colonizers and missionaries removed Indigenous children from their homes, they weren't just removing them from their families but robbing them of the critical education they would have received at home, which taught them who they were, their culture and their traditions, and the skills needed to live in the world.

LANGUAGE

As we get into the history of boarding schools later, it's critical for you to know the importance of language. Before colonization, over five hundred distinct languages were spoken in North America. These languages are grouped into language families, and each group can be wildly different from the next.

Most of us don't think about it often, but language is more than just the words that we speak. This is especially true when talking about people who primarily use oral traditions to pass on knowledge. Every word has a meaning that connects it to how we think about a thing. Even the number of words we have for something reflects how often we discuss it, like how the Iñupiat people of Alaska have over fifty words to describe snow.

When we talk about children having their Indigenous languages taken from them in boarding school, it isn't just about making them speak English. It's the destruction of the culture and worldview, or way of looking at the world, contained within their native tongue.

CAHOKIA

Cahokia was a bustling prehistoric city situated near the confluence of the Mississippi, Missouri, and Illinois Rivers. At its peak, around the year 1100 CE, it was one of the largest cities in the Americas, boasting a population potentially as high as twenty thousand people. The city was a hub for trade and commerce, with goods such as obsidian and copper being exchanged among the inhabitants and travelers alike. Archaeologists believe that Cahokia was a cosmopolitan city where different cultures met and mingled.

One of the most fascinating aspects of Cahokia is the sophisticated way its inhabitants altered the landscape. They built enormous earthworks, including platform mounds upon which they erected important buildings like temples and chiefs' residences. The largest of these mounds, Monks Mound, covers over fourteen acres and stands a hundred feet high. It's the largest prehistoric earthen construction in the Americas north of Mexico.

Cahokia wasn't just a city of commerce and impressive construction. It was also a city of invention. The people of Cahokia invented a game we now call "chunkey," which involved rolling a disc-shaped stone

A rendering by artist L. K. Townsend of what Cahokia looked like.

across a field and throwing spears to try to strike it. This game was so popular that it spread across the continent and was played by Indigenous peoples for hundreds of years.

By the end of the 1200s, Cahokia's population started to decline. The reasons for this are not fully understood but could include factors such as change in the flood patterns of the surrounding rivers. Although the city was eventually abandoned, Cahokia's unique mounds remain as reminders of the incredible civilization that once thrived there. Today, it is a UNESCO World Heritage Site that continues to teach us about the rich cultural heritage of the Indigenous peoples of North America.

LET'S THINK ABOUT THIS:

1. Which of these facts about Indigenous life have you learned before? What is new to you?
2. How does your life sound different from the lives of Indigenous people in the Americas before Europeans arrived?
3. Who in your community is responsible for your education? Your parents, your teachers, or someone else?

CHAPTER 2

THE ARRIVAL OF EUROPEANS

WHAT IS COLONIZATION?

Colonization is the process of people seeking to occupy and gain political power over a place. Colonizers sometimes act on their own, looking for a new area where they can have religious or cultural freedom or where they can make a living for themselves. Throughout history, colonizers have often acted on behalf of their home country or religious group. Once they travel to a new area, they create a community or settlement, called a "colony." That colony then becomes a cultural and religious outpost of their homeland.

The problem, of course, is that there are often

people already living on the lands that settlers want to colonize. Because of this, the history of colonization around the world is tied to violence and genocide, usually committed against Indigenous peoples. How would you feel if someone moved into your house and called it their own, then expected you to leave? No one wants to be removed from the place they know and love.

Colonization, remember, doesn't mean just moving into a place but establishing power over it. As colonizers formed settlements, they didn't include Indigenous people in decision-making processes or governments. In fact, they often feared their new Indigenous neighbors and sought to convert them to Christianity or displace them entirely.

The colonial era—the time when European colonizers began to arrive in the Americas—was plagued with violence, genocide, slavery, and disease. In the centuries that followed the initial arrival of Europeans, relationships between tribes and the British, French, and Spanish colonizers varied dramatically across regions, tribes, and trade networks.

In 1494, Spain and Portugal signed the Treaty of Tordesillas, which divided up newly "discovered" lands by drawing a line in the Atlantic Ocean from north to south, with the Spanish claiming all the land to the west of the line. The Spanish claimed dominion, or the right by God, to a large portion of the Americas—most of which they didn't know existed yet. The Portuguese were allowed to claim what would become Brazil. They began to enslave Africans and send them to toil in the fields of their plantations.

Spanish conquistadors used violence to lead a campaign of genocide through the territories they had claimed as their own. Armed with guns, cannons, and steel weapons, small groups of conquistadors devastated Indigenous communities and the empires of the Inca and Aztec. An estimated 240,000 Aztecs died during the siege of Tenochtitlán, the Aztec city where Mexico City is today.

The Spanish would continue to traverse the Americas, including large portions of what are now the southern United States. For many tribes in that area, their first contact with Europeans was with the Spanish, including the expeditions of conquistadors like Juan Ponce de León, Hernando de Soto, and Francisco Vázquez de Coronado.

Following initial exploration, Spanish missionaries established missions, places meant for the religious indoctrination and conversion of Indigenous people. From present-day California to Texas to Florida, missions began to pop up.

It wouldn't be until 1524 when another European country, France, would begin its own campaign to colonize North America. Following the failure of the Roanoke Colony in 1587, the English didn't begin another colonial project in the Americas until 1606, when King James granted a charter to the Virginia Company for a settlement at Jamestown, in present-day Virginia. In 1620, a group of Puritans known as the Pilgrims arrived in present-day Massachusetts and established the Plymouth Colony.

The first settlers to come to the Atlantic coast of what is now the United States wanted two things: land for farming and religious freedom. Unlike the large civilizations the Spanish conquistadors had encountered to the south, tribes in North America lived in smaller communities. While early relationships between tribes and the newly forming settlements could be friendly, there would also occasionally be violent encounters, with the violence coming from both settlers and Indigenous people.

While all this history happened before the existence of boarding schools, learning it will help explain why the boarding schools were eventually created. Before we get there, let's talk about why Europeans felt entitled to the land.

DIVINE RIGHT

Catholics and Christians in the colonial era believed that it was their duty to try to convert people to their religion. The pope, the head of the Catholic church, said in 1493 that if an explorer landed in a foreign place, they had the right to claim that place in the name of a Catholic monarch—the king or queen of a European country. This philosophy meant that most European Christians and Catholics believed that land not occupied by people of their faith, especially non-Christian people, whom they saw as "heathens," was open for them to take. They believed they had "divine right" to the land, that their God willed them to take it.

Armed with that idea, part of what we now call "the Doctrine of Discovery," Europeans continued, for hundreds of years, colonizing, or taking over, lands all around the world that were already inhabited by Indigenous people. Sometimes they would use violence to subjugate Indigenous populations, and once they had achieved stability, they would begin what is called "missionary work," the process of trying to convert people to Christianity. Churches from many denominations (groups who interpret the same religion in different ways) back across the ocean in Europe gave money to support this missionary work.

As missionaries made first contact with Indigenous Americans, they believed it was their job to begin to try to convert tribes to Christianity. As they traveled to areas across the Americas that hadn't yet been explored by other Europeans, missionaries frequently encountered tribes that had recently faced great losses in population from the diseases that had spread quickly across the continent following the initial arrival of Europeans.

What Is the Doctrine of Discovery?

While the colonization of the Americas began in 1492, the path for it was made by Pope Nicholas V, arguably the most powerful man on earth at the time, forty years before Columbus landed. In a document called *Dum Diversas*, the pope and the Catholic Church laid out the foundations of what would come to be known as the Doctrine of Discovery.

In a series of three major documents, called "papal bulls," the Catholic Church declared that any land not inhabited by European Christians was open for discovery and claim by Christian rulers. This allowed the kings and queens of countries like the United Kingdom and Spain to claim areas around the world as their own, and to take the land and resources of the Indigenous people living there.

Basically, the pope said Indigenous people didn't have rights to their own land because they weren't Catholic. European explorers like Christopher Columbus and Hernán Cortés used the Doctrine of Discovery as justification to abuse, enslave, and murder Indigenous inhabitants of the places they landed. The explorers didn't see the Indigenous peoples' existing societies, cultures, and governments as valid or equal to their own. Instead, they viewed these lands as "empty" and ready for their taking—all because Indigenous people didn't worship the same god as them.

This doctrine was the foundation for the political relationship between the U.S. government and tribes in the United States. It was never meant to keep Indigenous people safe and healthy or preserve the sovereignty of tribes. It was made to allow for the taking of the land and resources of Indigenous people.

The Doctrine of Discovery had devastating

impacts on Indigenous people around the world, from Africa to the South Pacific. In 2023, Pope Francis repudiated, or formally disagreed with, the papal bulls, and said that the taking of land and resources of Indigenous people wasn't part of the Catholic faith. But nothing can undo the damage that was done.

UNIMAGINABLE LOSS

Even with the intentional violence used by European colonizers, the largest cause of death for Indigenous people in the Americas was disease. Europeans lived in cities with animals and poor sanitation. They had trade networks across Asia and Africa and had spent millennia developing immune systems that were resilient to disease. Since Indigenous Americans were cut off from most of the world and didn't have livestock that spread diseases from humans to animals, they didn't have the same sort of immunity.

When Europeans arrived, the diseases they brought with them spread faster than they did. Because no one in that period—neither the colonizers nor Indigenous peoples—knew what germs were, diseases were often unknowingly spread from tribe to tribe and were often seen as a punishment for a community's misdeeds. The trade networks of Native American tribes were vast, so diseases spread quickly from the places where Europeans arrived to the far reaches of the Americas. It was truly devastating.

Upon the initial arrival of Christopher Columbus in 1492, about 60.5 million Indigenous people lived in the Western Hemisphere, around 10 percent of the world's population at the time. There were large civilizations with bustling cities, like Cuzco, the capital of the Incan Empire, or Tenochtitlán, the capital of the Aztecs. But people living in these cities still lacked the immunity to most European diseases. After colonization, the Indigenous population of the Americas plummeted, with as much as 90 percent of the population dying from waves of disease.

Some of the earliest missionaries to travel the Americas observed and documented communities that would go on to be destroyed by the time the next European arrived. Smallpox, typhus, and measles are thought to have been the leading cause of death. Because most Indigenous people used oral histories rather than written language, we can only guess at how terrifying this was for Indigenous people as it happened.

The survivors of these new diseases were left to do all the work of feeding and caring for their community. Fields still needed to be plowed, fish caught, corn harvested, but there were far fewer people to do it. When Europeans started to colonize the Americas and moved farther and farther away from the coasts, many Indigenous communities were suffering. They were vulnerable to being enslaved, displaced, or swindled out of land or resources.

What Is a Missionary?

A missionary is a person who travels to different places, usually far from where they live, with the purpose of converting people to their religion. They tell people about their own faith or religion but also do things like teach people or provide medical care. Often, missionaries built permanent settlements called "missions" and became the first Europeans to live among Indigenous people.

During the colonial era, missionaries came from countries across Europe, like England, France, Spain, and Portugal. They came from not only different countries but different sects, or groups, of the Christian faith. Catholics are one of the largest groups of Christians, and many Catholic missionaries, often from a group called "Jesuits," came to the Americas. Throughout the history of the colonies and America, many Christian groups, like Puritans, Quakers, Methodists, Mennonites, and Evangelicals, would go on to run missions and religious boarding schools for Indigenous children.

MISSION SCHOOLS AND PRAYING TOWNS

Missionaries arriving in the Americas were focused on converting Indigenous people to Christianity. The new white European settlers believed that because Indigenous people weren't Christian like them, they were inferior, even less than human.

As part of their mission to convert the Indigenous population, it was important for missionaries to develop written versions of Indigenous languages. They would learn an Indigenous language, document the grammar, record the vocabulary, and translate religious texts into the language of the people they were preaching to. Because of this, the first written text in many Indigenous languages is the Bible.

Mission activities also included educating children in both European languages and religion. As early as 1523, Franciscan missionaries arriving in North America established primary schools in the Spanish colonies of Mexico. In 1536, they formally established a school for the children of Aztec nobles, coining it Colegio de Santa Cruz de Tlatelolco, in an area of what we now call Mexico City.

The first mission school for Indigenous people in the British colonies in North America was established in 1634 by Father Andrew White, a Jesuit priest. In the area that is now southern Maryland, White founded St. Mary's mission and began to educate the Piscataway children from tribes surrounding the community. The Piscataway tribe were already

A 1694 engraving depicting Father Andrew White baptizing Chief Kittamaquund, a Piscataway warrior.

trading partners with the English settlers in the area, and their tayac, or chief, had recently converted to Christianity.

In 1646, missionary John Eliot preached his first sermon to an audience of Massachusett and Nipmuc men near the Massachusetts Bay Colony. Soon after these sermons began, fourteen towns were created for "praying Indians." These towns had churches and schools that sought to "civilize" the tribes. The tribes that Eliot was preaching to were incredibly vulnerable, as they had suffered a significant drop in their populations caused by disease that had spread in the decades before the towns were formed. Almost all of the remaining Massachusett people converted to Christianity.

The nearby Harvard College opened the Harvard Indian School in 1656, and in 1661, it used John Eliot's translation to print a Bible in Massachusett, the first Bible printed in an Indigenous language in North America.

As European colonization continued to spread, the foreign governments who had claimed pieces of the Americas as their own—the French, British, and Spanish—allowed the Catholic Church and various Christian sects to open up more and more missions and mission schools across the Americas. Some

Indigenous people willingly chose to send their children. At that time, most young people, white or Indigenous, didn't have the opportunity to go to school, so some parents wanted their children to go to learn to read and write, learn about religion, or even just receive a meal. Others reluctantly sent their children to school, believing that in order to survive along with new settlers, they would need to learn their ways.

THE FUR TRADE

Besides missionaries, conquistadors, and religious settlers, some of the other first Europeans to come to North America were British and French fur traders. Fur traders were eager to get their hands on the resources in this "new world." It may seem strange to us, but at the time, the fur trade was the largest, most profitable industry in the world. Many of the animals with the most valuable fur, like beavers, had been hunted to extinction in Europe, so fur companies came to North America to find more.

Because Indigenous people had expert knowledge of the land and animal behaviors, they were critical partners in the fur trade. They hunted and trapped animals to exchange their fur for goods like fabric, tools, weapons, coffee, and tobacco. Fur traders would bring the furs back to Europe to be turned into things like top hats, the finest of which were made from naturally waterproof beaver fur.

Because it benefited them financially, fur traders had good reason to maintain a positive relationship with Indigenous people. Unlike the religious groups on the east coast of America or the British colonists, fur traders—especially the French—weren't usually interested in building large settlements. And since there were fewer of them, they often spent more time with the Indigenous populations, with many even choosing to marry Indigenous women.

The fur trade was not simply a business. The goods that tribes traded for fur significantly altered traditional ways of life, influencing everything from methods of hunting to styles of dress. It disrupted traditional economic systems and trade networks, leading to an increased reliance on European goods. Overhunting to meet the demand for furs also disrupted ecosystems and led to the depletion of certain animal populations.

It also resulted in tense political relationships. Some tribes aligned with the French, while others partnered with the British, leading to a complex web of loyalties and conflicts. During this era, the alliances and rivalries formed significantly influenced territorial control and political power in North America.

The fur trade also contributed to an increase in conflict and warfare among tribes. Competition for control of the profitable fur trade led to violence. The introduction of firearms by the Europeans further escalated these conflicts and altered traditional warfare tactics.

Over time, the fur trade began to become less important—fashions changed, and the demand for fur began to decline. People no longer wanted Indigenous people as trading partners as much as they wanted the land that they lived on.

LET'S THINK ABOUT THIS:

1. Why did Europeans believe they were better than Indigenous people?
2. What important documents made colonizers believe they had the right to the land?
3. How did new diseases from Europe prevent Indigenous people from resisting colonization?

CHAPTER 3

TOWARD REVOLUTION

One of the first large conflicts between the colonizers, the French and Indian War, took place between 1754 and 1763. The fight was to prevent British expansion into the Ohio River Valley, and it was also part of a larger war between Britain and France called the Seven Years' War. Many tribes, like the Algonquin, Lenape, Wyandot, Anishinaabe, Odawa, Shawnee, and the Mi'kmaq, fought on the side of the French. The six nations of the Haudenosaunee (ho-dah-nuh-show-nee) Confederacy, the Mohawk, Oneida, Onondaga, Cayuga, Tuscarora, and Seneca, fought on the side of the British.

Beyond the losses of battle, the Native warriors also suffered tremendously from disease. Smallpox, an incredibly contagious and often deadly disease, spread quickly. While almost all the French and British soldiers had immunity from the disease, the Native warriors were unprotected. As they returned home, they spread the disease to their communities, completely wiping out the population of some Odawa villages. The smallpox outbreak, along with brutal British warfare tactics like burning the homes and crops of the Native Americans fighting on the side of the French, created a turning point in the war, as tribes became unwilling to continue fighting alongside the Europeans while suffering such losses.

By 1760, fighting between the French and British ended in North America, but continued on in England and France. When the Seven Years' War concluded with the Treaty of Paris in 1763, the French were forced to give up control of all land east of the Mississippi, and to let the British have Canada.

Many tribes were not happy with the new situation. The French had a strong relationship built on trading with tribes in the Great Lakes area, and they didn't often bring settlers onto the lands that the tribes lived on. The British were very different, bringing in waves of settlers who were hungry for land and resources. These new settlers kept pushing westward, farther and farther into tribal lands.

While the French had seen most Indigenous people as allies and invested in maintaining good relations, the British saw Indigenous people as subjects, and stopped upholding the important traditions that had held together positive relationships with tribes. Because the war had been so expensive and the British were in a lot of debt, they dramatically decreased the number of gifts they gave to tribal leaders. The exchange of gifts wasn't just about the things being gifted, but about being in a respectful relationship. This disrespect, along with the rising population of settlers, led to tribal leaders feeling increasingly frustrated.

In 1761, with tensions increasing, Seneca leaders began to call for war on the British. The British discovered this plot and thought that tribes decided against acting. But they were only waiting. Support for war began to grow, as a Lenni Lenape prophet named Neolin spread the word of a vision he had, that their creator, the Master of Life, wanted tribes to push the white men out of their lands and back to Europe. He believed that tribes were being punished for trading with the white man and giving up their traditional ways.

The following year, Odawa chief Pontiac used this prophecy to bring together a half dozen tribes, some unlikely allies, to stand up against British domination. During this event, called Pontiac's Uprising, the tribes began burning the houses of settlers near British forts. This caused the forts to become crowded, and smallpox began to spread.

On June 24, 1763, tribal leaders visited Fort Pitt, urging the British to leave the area, but the British refused. As they left, the British did something unthinkable. William Trent, a former Indian agent and militia captain, wrote about this in his journal: "Out of our regard for them, we gave them two blankets and a handkerchief out of the smallpox hospital. I hope it will have the desired effect."

This kind of germ warfare is now a war crime—something that world governments have agreed not to subject people to because of its cruelty. But the event was not a one-off. Sir Jeffery Amherst, commander of the British forces, wrote in a letter: "Could it not be contrived to send the smallpox among those disaffected tribes of Indians? We must, on this occasion, use every stratagem in our power to reduce them." A wave of smallpox spread through the region, although it is impossible to prove the connection to the incident at Fort Pitt.

While this stage of the rebellion was quelled by the arrival of many more British troops, an official peace treaty with Chief Pontiac wouldn't be signed until 1766. The aftermath of the rebellion, which had killed over two thousand settlers (deaths of Indigenous people went undocumented) left colonists increasingly frustrated with the British colonial government, and increasingly hostile to Indigenous people.

TIME FOR REVOLUTION

King George III wrote the Royal Proclamation of 1763, declaring an Indian reserve along the Appalachian Mountains, as a border for white settlement to stop. It seemed like a good thing at the time. The proclamation stated that Native Americans "who live under our Protection, should not be molested or disturbed" and told colonists not to take their lands or buy them without getting permission from the government.

Of course, many colonists did not like this new restriction. They wanted land, and they felt like they deserved it. If there were Indigenous people on it, they didn't care. They were willing to fight for the land they now saw as theirs with violence, which was often aimed at tribes that had been peaceful neighbors.

Restrictions placed upon the colonists by a king far across the ocean did not go over well. They didn't want anyone telling them where they could live. And they were angry about the growing number of new taxes imposed upon them, among other grievances. So, on July 4, 1776, the thirteen colonies declared their independence from Great Britain. In the Declaration of Independence, Thomas Jefferson called Indigenous people "merciless Indian savages" and blamed King George for not doing more to protect colonists from them.

The Revolutionary War began. During the war, there were over eighty distinct tribes living east of the Mississippi. Every tribe chose different actions, with some remaining neutral and some choosing a side. Many tribes saw an independent United States as a bigger threat than the British, because the British had set boundaries on westward expansion.

The war ended with the Treaty of Paris establishing American independence in 1783. It was negotiated with no input from tribes on either side. For some tribes, like the Kanyen'keha:ka (Mohawk), siding with the British meant an almost complete loss of their lands. American independence would impact all tribes within its growing borders, as a new era began.

What Are Treaties?

Treaties are legally binding documents that define the relationships between governments. In the context of this book, treaties were made between the federal government and tribes. Article I, Section 8, of the Constitution gives Congress the sole right to negotiate treaties with tribes. Between 1777 and 1871, around 370 treaties were ratified by the U.S. Senate, while forty-five more were negotiated with tribes but never ratified.

These treaties don't give tribes rights; they protect the rights that tribes already had before colonization and set out the responsibilities the government owes to a tribe. They lay out a set of promises between two governments. Many treaties guarantee rights to harvest food, fish, or hunt. They may guarantee a supply of food, health care, or education.

While tribes ceded large amounts of land in many of the treaties negotiated with the United States, the federal government has not done a good job at holding up its end of the bargain, often failing to provide resources or not honoring the rights of Indigenous people.

It is important to remember that while these treaties were negotiated a long time ago, they are still valid, and the federal government must still honor their terms.

ERAS OF FEDERAL INDIAN POLICY

To understand why the boarding school system was created, it's important to understand how the U.S. government has been in relationship with Indigenous people since its founding. The rules that dictate this relationship are called "federal Indian policy" and have changed through time; it can be helpful to think about different "eras" of federal Indian policy. Each one of these eras changed life for Indigenous people, and impacted Indigenous children, in different ways:

1. **COEXISTENCE ERA (1770s–1820s)**: During this era, the U.S. government signed treaties with tribes

with the overall intention to get tribes to exchange their land for money and goods.

2. **REMOVAL ERA (1830s–1850s):** The U.S. government decided to displace tribes, forcing them to move away from their homes to make room for new settlers.
3. **RESERVATION ERA (1850s–1890s):** The government made tribes move onto specific areas of land, called "reservations." Tribes were led to believe that this would protect their access to food, water, and other resources, but it led to many tribes losing their homelands and all access to the ways of life that had been familiar to them.
4. **ASSIMILATION ERA (1880s–1930s):** In this period, the federal government tried to force Indigenous people to adopt white Christian customs and the English language. This is the period during which most boarding schools were created, as they were meant to further the policy of assimilation, erasing Indigenous culture and language.
5. **REORGANIZATION ERA (1930s–1950s):** The government realized the assimilation policy was failing and tried to force tribes to govern their own people in a way that was dictated by the federal government.
6. **TERMINATION ERA (1950s–1960s):** The government attempted to end, or "terminate," its recognition of

Native American tribes as separate nations. This resulted in many tribes losing their lands and their rights, and many Indigenous people being told to relocate to major cities, and further loss of culture and community.

7. **SELF-DETERMINATION ERA (1960s–TODAY):** Due to the actions of Indigenous activists, the federal government recognized that Indigenous people have the right to govern themselves. Despite this, the government still has policies in place that limit the ability for Indigenous people and tribes to thrive.

These eras can help us understand the history of Indigenous people in the Americas and their ongoing fight for rights and recognition.

LET'S THINK ABOUT THIS:

1. Why did some tribes unite during Pontiac's Uprising?
2. Why might Indigenous people today not feel included in the Declaration of Independence?
3. Why would tribes sign treaties with the government?

CHAPTER 4

AMERICA

Following the Revolutionary War, Henry Knox, the first secretary of war for the United States, knew it was important to make peace with Native nations. In 1786, Secretary Knox warned against the idea of taking land by force and recommended that the U.S. government continue making treaties with the tribes that allowed them to buy land, like the British had done. This helped Americans get land without going to war again.

Following Knox's way, the government made a plan for how to treat tribes and included it in a document called the Northwest Ordinance of 1787. This plan, which was made into law on July 13, 1787, was the first official rule for how the U.S. would deal with Indigenous people.

Article 3 of the ordinance stated:

> *Religion, morality, and knowledge, being necessary to good government and the happiness of mankind, schools and the means of education shall forever be encouraged. The utmost good faith shall always be observed towards the Indians; their lands and property shall never be taken from them without their consent; and in the property, rights, and liberty, they shall never be invaded or disturbed, unless in just and lawful wars authorized by Congress; but laws founded in justice and humanity, shall from time to time be made for preventing wrongs being done to them, and for preserving peace and friendship with them.*

Unfortunately, even though this was now the law of the land, it didn't stop many settlers from continuing to push farther westward, often treating the Indigenous people living where they settled with violence and disrespect.

Meanwhile, a group of (all white and male) new Americans sat down in Philadelphia to write the Constitution. They had many governments from around the world to look to for inspiration for how their new republic should function. But one group they drew many ideas from was pretty close to home: the Haudenosaunee Confederacy. Sometimes called the Iroquois Confederacy, it is made up of six nations: the Kanyen'keha:ka (Mohawk), Onayotekaono (Oneida), Onundagaono (Onondaga), Guyohkohnyoh (Cayuga), Onondowahgah (Seneca), and Skaruhreh (Tuscarora). While the Tuscarora joined the confederacy in 1722, the first five nations have been an alliance since time immemorial (before written history), making it the longest-standing participatory democracy in the world. Each tribe has its own unique language and culture, and they are allied together under the Great Law of Peace. Each tribe has representatives to the Grand Council, which then makes decisions by consensus, where representatives discuss and vote on issues that come before them. The Haudenosaunee are still allied today.

Many of the men attending the Constitutional Convention, including John Adams, Thomas Jefferson, and Benjamin Franklin, were familiar with the system because they had negotiated treaties with the confederacy.

The Haudenosaunee had different leaders for the army and the government. They protected some personal freedoms, like freedom of religion, and had some democratic rules for voting, saying no to ideas, and removing leaders from power. While the writers of the Constitution would use these ideas in their document, they didn't include a critical part of the Haudenosaunee system—the inclusion of women.

Despite this influence, no Indigenous leaders were involved in the writing of the Constitution. In fact, the document uses language that makes it clear that Native tribes and their citizens existed outside the system the writers of the Constitution were building.

Section 8, Clause 3 of the Constitution gives Congress the power "to regulate Commerce with foreign Nations, and among the several States, and with the Indian Tribes." This means that Indigenous tribes are as important as states and other countries. It means Indigenous nations have similar powers and rights to any nation. This lets tribal nations have a lot of power over their own rule—a concept that we call "sovereignty."

It also means that Indigenous people were not made citizens of the United States, so they wouldn't have any power to vote in elections. In fact, it would be 137 years until Indigenous Americans would become citizens.

REGULATING TRADE

Just two months after Rhode Island became the final state to ratify the Constitution, the newly formed Congress passed its first major piece of federal Indian policy—the Trade and Intercourse Act of 1790. The law placed almost all trade with Indigenous people under the control of the federal government. There would eventually be six Trade and Intercourse Acts.

This first law set up a system to acquire Indigenous lands through treaties, created the position of Indian agents (whose job it was to work with tribes), outlined punishments for crimes committed against and by Indigenous people, and asserted the government's commitment to "civilizing the Indians."

What Does It Mean to "Civilize" Someone?

The idea of being "civilized" in American history is often very Eurocentric—which means it's seen from a white, European perspective. In the eighteenth century, many white people thought Europeans were better than "colored" or "savage" people, like Africans or Indigenous people from around the world. They thought cultures that were unlike theirs were less advanced, and discounted non-white systems of knowledge. This led to them trying to make those cultures act like white Europeans and European-born Americans.

In the United States, this meant teaching Indigenous people about Christianity, convincing them to depend on European methods of agriculture, educating them in English-speaking schools, and more. By saying that the white, European way of life was "civilized" and more moral, or good, early Americans were able to justify their treatment of Indigenous people. In their minds, they weren't taking away the rich cultures, histories, and knowledge of groups of people, but bringing those people into the modern era.

We know now that this idea of what it means to be civilized isn't just wrong; it's very racist. Racism is when some people believe that one race is better than another. This can lead to treating people unfairly because of their race. It happens in areas like the legal system, schools, jobs, and homes. For example, if a teacher doesn't let certain students take harder classes because of their race, that's racist. It's not fair to the student and stops them from doing their best in school.

Non-European cultures had their own ways of passing on knowledge, history, and values, as well as incredibly complex systems of governance, agriculture, land management, and more. Just because their lives and societies were different doesn't mean they were less advanced. In fact, we're still learning just how many Indigenous technologies were better for people, animals, and the planet than the systems imposed in their place.

SNEAKY MOTIVES

While this time in the relationship between tribes and the government was relatively peaceful, the real intention of many American leaders was still to take the land of tribes and keep them moving west. The man who wrote the Declaration of Independence and our third president, Thomas Jefferson, is a good example. While he often publicly touted the importance of peace with the tribes, he wrote privately in 1803 to William Henry Harrison, who would become our ninth president, about his true intentions. In his letter,

President Jefferson outlines his plan to take the land of tribes who aren't willing to relocate from lands that Americans want: to use trading houses (stores where Indigenous people would go to trade for imported goods—the Target or Walmart of their time) to get Indigenous people into debt. Then, when they didn't have the money to pay their debts, tribes would be pushed to surrender their lands to cover the balance.

He plotted that when enough Indigenous people were pushed to sell their lands this way, and as white settlers began to move in, the remaining Indigenous people would either want to become American citizens or they would move west of the Mississippi River.

Pointing out that it was important that the tribes fear Americans, Jefferson wrote a very scary sentence: "[The Indians] must see we have only to shut our hand to crush them and that all our liberalities to them proceed from motives of pure humanity only." Basically, the tribes should know that Americans are only choosing to treat them humanely because they are behaving in the way the colonizers like and if they try to resist, their people will either be removed from their lands or killed.

This scheme immediately impacted tribes, as you can read in the many treaties from the time period. Tribes, who had become dependent on the goods that they traded for, were forced to sell their lands or sign treaties ceding it to cover their debts to the trading houses.

LOUISIANA PURCHASE

Just months after writing his letter to William Henry Harrison, President Jefferson would learn that his representatives in Paris were able to buy the entire Louisiana Territory from France.

The United States had paid about four cents for each acre of 828,000 square miles of land west of the Mississippi River. With the stroke of a pen, the United States got twice as big, growing the country farther toward the west.

The Louisiana Purchase ignored the well-being and desires of the tribes that were already living on that land and made settlers even hungrier for more territory. Most Americans at that time used land for growing crops, harvesting timber, and raising cattle, and they saw the presence of Indigenous people as a barrier to their livelihoods. They felt like they deserved the land more than the tribes did, because they saw the Indigenous way of life as less valuable than theirs.

Why did settlers feel like they had the right to make tribes move? It was rooted in a concept called "Manifest Destiny."

Manifest Destiny was an idea that was deeply ingrained in the minds of many Americans in the nineteenth century. It was the belief that the United States was destined, even ordained by God, to expand its boundaries and spread its form of democracy from the Atlantic Ocean to the Pacific. This concept was coined by a newspaper editor named John L. O'Sullivan in 1845, but the concept was a central idea in the founding of the United States.

The concept of Manifest Destiny was not just about getting more land. It was also linked to several other ideas. One of these was the belief in what would later be called "American exceptionalism," the idea that America was a unique nation, a beacon of freedom and democracy. Proponents of Manifest Destiny believed it was the duty of white Americans to spread their culture and religion as far as they could.

This belief system influenced many American policies and shaped the nation's behavior. It was used to justify the annexation of Texas, the acquisition of Oregon, and the Mexican-American War, which resulted in the United States gaining California and much of the Southwest. The idea also played a role in the removal of tribes from their lands.

Not everyone agreed with the concept of Manifest Destiny at the time, but those who didn't were in the great minority. They might have seen Manifest

Destiny as an excuse for American imperialism (the desire to dominate other people and lands) and a way to justify horrible treatment of Black and Indigenous people. These critics argued that the idea was a form of racism and that it led to displacement and suffering.

Manifest Destiny had significant consequences for tribes. It was used to justify genocidal policies, like forced relocation and, eventually, boarding schools.

THE INDIAN CIVILIZATION ACT

In 1819, Congress passed the Indian Civilization Act, which gave "benevolent societies," meaning churches and missions, funds to "civilize" Indigenous children by teaching them reading and writing and converting them to Christianity.

The biggest champion of this act was a Quaker man named Thomas Loraine McKenney, who was the head of the Office of Indian Trade. In 1824, when the Bureau of Indian Affairs was established, McKenney was appointed as the superintendent of Indian Affairs.

From his new post, McKenney advocated for the "civilization" program. Between 1819 and 1830, fifty-two schools were opened and received funding under the Indian Civilization Act. At the time, these schools were located near tribal communities. But the idea that Indigenous people could assimilate and live peacefully alongside their white neighbors was growing less and less popular, and the settlers' desire for the lands where tribes were living was growing more intense.

In a speech to Congress in 1825, President James Monroe spoke about moving tribes to lands west of the Mississippi River. He agreed that Indigenous people couldn't become part of white culture. He said it would be better for the tribes to leave their lands, for their own good.

> *The removal of the tribes from the territory which they now inhabit . . . would not only shield them from impending ruin, but promote their welfare and happiness. Experience has clearly demonstrated that in their present state it is impossible to incorporate them in such masses, in any form whatever, into our system. It has also demonstrated with equal certainty that without a timely anticipation of and provision against the dangers to which they are exposed, under causes which it will be difficult, if not impossible, to control, their degradation and extermination will be inevitable.*

LET'S THINK ABOUT THIS:

1. Why do you think that the founders of the United States didn't include Indigenous people as citizens in the Constitution?
2. Was Thomas Jefferson a friend to Indigenous people?
3. How does Manifest Destiny connect to the Doctrine of Discovery as it is described in chapter two?

BE STRONG, AHYOKA

The year was 1838, and it was a cold winter in the heart of the Cherokee homelands, in the place we now call Tennessee. Nestled among the forests and rolling hills lived an eleven-year-old girl named Ahyoka. She was an energetic child with bright eyes and a smile that could bring light to the gloomiest of days. Ahyoka lived with her grandmother Woya in a cabin made of logs, surrounded by the sights and sounds of nature.

Life for Ahyoka was full of work but also full of joy. She spent her days cooking, sewing, exploring the woods, listening to the stories passed down by her elders, and helping Woya tend to their large garden. Some days, they would go into the hills to gather wild berries, herbs, and nuts, sharing laughter as they worked side by side.

One fateful day, their peaceful life was shattered by the arrival of a group of American soldiers on horseback. They came with orders from their president to remove the Cherokee from their homes and relocate them to a faraway place. Ahyoka clung to her grandmother, her heart heavy with fear and uncertainty.

The chief of her people led the community in prayer as they were forced to leave behind their homes, most of their belongings, and everything they held dear. Ahyoka watched in disbelief as the people of their village loaded what they could into wagons.

One very old man stood at his door and asked a soldier to allow him time to pray with his family in their home, one last time before they left. The answer came swiftly, as the soldier shouted, "No! No time for prayers. Go!" while pushing the feeble man out of the house. With a heavy heart, Ahyoka and Woya joined the long line of their family and neighbors, embarking on a journey that would come to be known as the Trail of Tears.

They walked for weeks on end, their weary feet trudging through cold mud and rain. Ahyoka complained, angry and confused about how long this horrible experience would continue. But as conditions began to grow worse, her grandmother told her she needed to be strong.

Ahyoka did her best to be brave and strong, but she began to notice that her grandmother was growing weaker with each passing mile. Her steps became slower, her breaths more labored. Ahyoka did everything she could to ease her grandmother's suffering, but she had little to offer other than words of comfort. So many of her people were sick now, so many had been lost; she prayed that her grandmother would survive.

Despite her prayers, Woya's health continued to deteriorate. One cold night, as they huddled together for warmth beneath a worn blanket, Ahyoka's grandmother spoke her final words, her voice barely a whisper in the howling wind.

"Remember who you are, Ahyoka."

With tears streaming down her cheeks, Ahyoka held Woya's frail hand in hers, feeling the weight of her loss like a heavy rock in her chest. As the first light of dawn painted the sky in hues of orange and gold, Ahyoka found her aunts and told them what had happened in the night. The family realized they had to leave her grandmother here, without a proper burial. Their hearts burst into pieces, but the soldiers forced them to start walking.

The perilous walk continued for what seemed like an eternity. Ahyoka cried more tears than she knew she could. Her feet were bruised and battered, but she had grown numb to the pain. Every day was full of hardships, but something kept her going. It was like she could feel her grandmother's hand on her back, steadying her.

And her people finally arrived at their new home. Ahyoka gazed out at the endless flat horizon stretching before her. She whispered a silent promise to Woya and all her friends and family who had been lost along the way—to never forget them, to always carry the flame of hope in her heart, no matter how dark the path ahead might seem.

CHAPTER 5

REMOVAL AND RESERVATIONS

After running for president in 1824 and losing, Andrew Jackson ran again in 1828. His opponents warned the American public that he was violent, bloodthirsty, and a tyrant in the making. Despite all this, and Jackson being the least qualified, least educated man to ever run for president until that point, he won the office easily, having more than twice the electoral votes of his competitor.

Removing Indigenous people from east of the Mississippi was his top priority when he took office. He laid out his plans in his first address to Congress in 1829:

> *This emigration should be voluntary, for it would be as cruel as unjust to compel the aborigines*

[Indigenous people] to abandon the graves of their fathers and seek a home in a distant land. But they should be distinctly informed that if they remain within the limits of the States, they must be subject to their laws. In return for their obedience as individuals they will without doubt be protected in the enjoyment of those possessions which they have improved by their industry. But it seems to me visionary to suppose that in this state of things claims can be allowed on tracts of country on which they have neither dwelt nor made improvements, merely because they have seen them from the mountain or passed them in the chase. Submitting to the laws of the States, and receiving, like other citizens, protection in their persons and property, they will ere long become merged in the mass of our population.

On May 28, 1830, President Jackson signed the Indian Removal Act and formally began the next era of federal Indian policy, known as the removal era. The Removal Act authorized the president to negotiate with tribes for new territory, west of the Mississippi River.

But of course, most tribes didn't want to go. Much of a tribe's culture and identity is, and was, deeply connected to the land, plants, and animals of their homelands. And beyond that, who would want to leave their house and way of life just so someone else could move in?

Unlike what he had said in his speech in 1829, Jackson didn't really care whether or not tribes wanted to leave.

What Are Reservations?

Reservations are lands that have been designated for the use of Indigenous tribes within the United States. The majority of reservations were created by treaties signed in the nineteenth century during the removal era. Reservations are incredibly small compared to the size of the original land bases that tribes inhabited, and moving to them severed important spiritual connections between Indigenous people and the land.

Because many are located far from the original homelands of tribes, they frequently presented tribes with environments that were totally unfamiliar to them. This forced tribes to dramatically change the lifestyles they had been accustomed to. Reservations were usually put in places with few resources, because they were less desirable to settlers. This often pushed tribes into precarious situations, sometimes leading to starvation and disease.

Reservations still exist today, and unlike in years past, Indigenous people are allowed to leave them. In fact, most Indigenous people in the United States today live in cities outside of the boundaries of the reservation where they are citizens.

THE FIVE CIVILIZED TRIBES AND THE TRAIL OF TEARS

The "Five Civilized Tribes" is a term used to describe five Indigenous nations—the Cherokee, Chickasaw, Choctaw, Creek (Muscogee), and Seminole—because they adopted numerous cultural and governmental practices of the European settlers during colonial and early American periods. These included using European farming techniques, wearing European-style dress, and owning enslaved people. They had their own newspapers written in their languages. In 1827, the Cherokee even drafted their own constitution.

But Americans were desperate to control the lands that belonged to the tribes. In 1828, there were reports of gold being found in the Cherokee homelands in what is now the northern part of Georgia. This caused a huge stir, and as news spread across the states, prospectors (people searching for gold) flooded onto Cherokee lands.

As Benjamin Parks, said to be the first person who discovered gold in this area, wrote in *The Atlanta Constitution* in 1894:

> *The news got abroad, and such excitement you never saw. It seemed within a few days as if the whole world must have heard of it, for men came from every state I had ever heard of. They came afoot, on horseback and in wagons, acting more like crazy men than anything else. All the way from where Dahlonega now stands to Nuckollsville [Auraria] there were men panning out of the branches and making holes in the hillsides.*

The gold rush only helped fuel the removal of the Cherokee from their lands. After the signing of the Indian Removal Act, and despite the efforts of the Five Civilized Tribes to adopt the ways of the settlers rapidly surrounding them, the tribes were forced to leave their homes.

The Choctaw were the first to be forcibly removed in 1831. The Muscogee and Creek tribe was forcibly removed in 1836, followed by the Chickasaw in 1837. In 1838, in an effort to remove the remaining Cherokees from their homelands, U.S. troops began the forced march of over sixteen thousand men, women, and children, an event which would come to be known as the Trail of Tears. The journey, which many people were forced to make barefoot and inadequately clothed for the cold and wet weather, took over three months to complete. Along the way, over four thousand Cherokee people died from illness and exposure to the harsh weather, while many faced violence from white settlers.

Many tribes across the country experienced forced migration similar to that of the Trail of Tears, in which they were removed from their homelands and forced onto small parcels of land in what was then called "Indian Territory" and is now the state of Oklahoma.

Why Did Tribes Sign Treaties?

While many tribes in both the British colonies and early America signed treaties giving up their lands in exchange for new ones, we know that they often did so under extreme pressure, threats of violence, and immense suffering. We also know that government agents often made promises to tribal leaders that they had no intention of keeping.

As Dr. Elden Lawrence of the Sisseton Wahpeton Dakota community said in 2010:

> *Everything that they used to get them to sign treaties, I think was illegal in a lot of ways—browbeating, brainwashing, and then on the other hand telling them, ". . . If you sign this treaty, you're not going to ever have to work or hunt again; we'll take care of you." Everything will be provided. Every year you'll get so much money to buy your needs, your pots and pans and stuff, but we'll also have food coming in every month, or once a year for you. The other alternative is . . . "We're going to drive you all the way to the Rocky Mountains where you're going to starve to death and we'll never have to worry about you again." Those were the conditions that were being talked about, and sometimes I think they might have done that.*

In many cases across the United States, Indigenous representatives who signed treaties did so without approval of a majority of their communities. This meant that their communities were often surprised to learn that a piece of paper gave settlers the right to their lands.

THE CIVIL WAR AND THE INDIAN WARS

In 1860, President Abraham Lincoln was elected, winning none of the Southern, slave-holding states. South Carolina became the first state to secede from the United States in December 1860. Eventually, eleven states would secede, forming the Confederacy. The Civil War began in 1861.

Most Indigenous people wanted to stay out of the war, but a small minority of wealthy, slave-holding tribal members from the Five Civilized Tribes signed treaties with the Confederate government and promised volunteers for their war effort. At the same time as these tribes sent thousands of men to fight on the side of the South,

Indigenous people from other tribes joined the Union effort.

In August of the following year, in Minnesota (which had just recently become a state), Dakota people, who had signed treaties placing them on reservations, were upset about the U.S. government not fulfilling the promises they'd made to them in exchange for their lands. With their children starving, several Dakota warriors, led by Chief Little Crow, attacked white settlements, killing 358 settlers. The U.S. government retaliated, holding all Dakota people in Minnesota responsible for the actions of a few.

In November, following months of conflict with the Dakota, U.S. soldiers rounded up over 1,658 Dakota people, mostly women and children, at the Lower Sioux Agency. More than three hundred Dakota men were held there to stand trial, while the remaining Dakota were marched to Fort Snelling, an over-one-hundred-mile journey that most did on foot in the Minnesota cold. The conditions at the prison camp established for them there were so harsh that as many as three hundred Dakota died over the winter.

On December 26, 1862, at the authorization of President Lincoln, thirty-eight Dakota men were hanged simultaneously in front of a large crowd in the city of Mankato. It remains the largest mass execution in U.S. history. Two additional Dakota warriors were found in Canada and hung at Fort Snelling. That spring, the Dakota remaining at Fort Snelling were exiled to Nebraska.

In response to the Dakota uprising, Congress passed laws nullifying U.S. treaties with the Dakota and making it illegal for Dakota people to live or own property in Minnesota. This law is no longer enforced, but remains on the books, a painful reminder to Dakota people today.

Throughout the West, the influx of new settlers and railroads pushed more and more tribes into conflict with the government, resulting in the horrific treatment of thousands of Indigenous people. One particularly horrible incident was the Sand Creek Massacre of 1864, which happened when a group of American soldiers attacked a peaceful group of Cheyenne and Arapaho people in Colorado. Even though the tribes were not at war with America, and even flew an American flag to show they were friendly, the soldiers brutally killed 230 Indigenous people, including women and children. No soldiers were held accountable or put on trial.

That same year, the U.S. military waged an especially violent campaign against the Diné (Navajo) people, killing their livestock, burning their villages, and murdering anyone who resisted. Over the course of the next two years, more than 10,000 Diné would be forced to march as far as 450 miles to Fort Sumner, with hundreds dying along the way. Overcrowding, intertribal conflicts, disease, and famine led to an additional 2,380 Diné and Mescalero Apache dying at the fort before being allowed to travel back to their homelands.

Attempts to render Indigenous people helpless continued in 1868, when the U.S. government paid settlers to kill herds of buffalo, which tribes depended on to survive. Hunters left the buffalo, which held spiritual importance to many tribes, to rot on the prairie. The buffalo were hunted to near extinction, cutting off a critical food source for Indigenous people.

In 1871, Congress ended the era of treaty making with Indigenous tribes. From then on, they would use laws passed by Congress and signed by the president to make policy having to do with the tribes.

THE GHOST DANCE AND THE WOUNDED KNEE MASSACRE

Even after decades of forcible relocation and losing vast portions of their homelands through treaties and allotment, the languages, cultures, and religions of Indigenous people continued to thrive. Native resistance could not be killed. Indigenous people from across the West began adopting the Ghost Dance, a religious movement that had been revived by a Paiute man named Wovoka. Wovoka had visions that showed that if Indigenous people performed the Ghost Dance, their ancestors would stop westward expansion, bring back the buffalo, and return all of America to Indigenous people.

Tribes across the West began to travel to listen to Wovoka, and brought the Ghost Dance back to their peoples. The Ghost Dance would last four days and was to be done every two months. Hundreds, or even thousands, of Indigenous people would participate.

This movement made the Bureau of Indian Affairs agents living on reservations very uneasy. They didn't like the idea of so many Indigenous people doing the dance. When the Ghost Dance spread to the Lakota, the BIA agents at the Pine Ridge Reservation called in the military and sent forty-three police officers to arrest Hunkpapa Lakota leader Sitting Bull. During the arrest, nine Hunkpapa, including Sitting Bull, were killed.

Following the murder of Sitting Bull, Spotted Elk, the leader of the Miniconjou Lakota, led 350 of his people to Pine Ridge, hoping to negotiate peace with the Americans. The military leaders there didn't trust his intentions, and on December 28, 1890, the Seventh Calvary met the group and led them toward Wounded Knee Creek. There were over 500 U.S. troops and only 350 Lakota, including 230 women and children.

Hunkpapa Lakota leader Sitting Bull in 1884.

On the morning of December 29, American soldiers conducted a search of the camp and confiscated 38 rifles that they had found. During the raid, there was a scuffle that led to a rifle being discharged by one of the Dakota. The Seventh Cavalry used this as an opportunity to start a full-on assault of the Dakota, most of whom had already been disarmed. They shot people down indiscriminately and used Hotchkiss guns (rotating cannons) to fire upon the tipis of Dakota women and children. Soldiers went after Dakota who fled, killing them at will. By the end, the Seventh Calvary had killed as many as 300 out of 350 Dakota. The Massacre at Wounded

Knee is still the deadliest mass shooting in American history.

Black Elk, an Oglala Lakota medicine man, recalled years later:

> *I did not know then how much was ended. When I look back now from this high hill of my old age, I can still see the butchered women and children lying heaped and scattered all along the crooked gulch as plain as when I saw them with eyes still young. And I can see that something else died there in the bloody mud, and was buried in the blizzard. A people's dream died there. It was a beautiful dream. And I, to whom so great a vision was given in my youth,—you see me now a pitiful old man who has done nothing, for the nation's hoop is broken and scattered. There is no center any longer, and the sacred tree is dead.*

LET'S THINK ABOUT THIS:

1. Were Indigenous people forcibly removed from the area where you live?
2. Do you know the names of the tribes who lived on the land that you do now? Do they still live there today?
3. Have you ever been to a reservation? Are there any located near your hometown?

CHAPTER 6

KILL THE INDIAN, SAVE THE MAN

By the 1880s, a growing number of people in New England were upset with how Indigenous people were being treated. They didn't see a way for American society to function if the only way of dealing with Indigenous people was through violence. They began to push for reforms in government policies toward tribes, so we call them "reformers."

While the reformers thought of themselves as "friends of the Indian," they still believed that white, Christian culture was superior to Indigenous cultures. They believed that Indigenous people had to be "saved from themselves" through government-supported efforts to assimilate them into white American society.

Their main ideas on how to do this were not

new. They wanted to remove Native children from reservation day schools, which the government had been funding since the early 1800s, and send them to schools far away from their reservations. Reformers wanted to break up tribal views about communal land ownership and values of interconnectedness, as they saw these things as major barriers to the assimilation of Indigenous people into American society. With this idea in mind, they helped push the Dawes Act, one of the most impactful pieces of federal Indian policy.

THE DAWES ACT

The Dawes Act, also known as the General Allotment Act, was a law passed in 1887 and signed by President Grover Cleveland. It aimed to assimilate Indigenous people into mainstream white American society by dividing up reservation lands into individual property. The government, and reformers, believed this would encourage the Indigenous people to adopt a lifestyle they deemed acceptable, where individual families would farm plots of land, giving up their traditional lifeways.

Lands that were once held collectively by tribes

were broken up into 160–320 acre sections called "allotments," which were to be used for farming or grazing animals. While the government and reformers claimed that allotment was done to protect the rights of Indigenous people to their own plots of land, it had a darker agenda. Any "surplus" land that was not given to the Indigenous people was sold to white settlers. The real objective of the Dawes Act was to open Western lands, which were largely populated by Indigenous people, to white settlement. This was a clear act of theft, denying tribes land they had been promised in treaties signed with the government.

By the early 1900s, the consequences of the Dawes Act became very clear. Indigenous peoples lost massive amounts of land. Of the 138 million acres of land tribes originally held, they were left with only 48 million acres. That's almost 65 percent of Indigenous land taken away in less than two decades.

A newspaper ad for sale of "Indian Land" across multiple states in 1911.

After the initial passage of the Dawes Act, the practice of allotment elevated frustrations of tribes, already upset with Americans over unkept promises in treaties and continued illegal occupation of their lands. Allotment had a significant and harmful impact on Indigenous peoples. It forced a lifestyle change on them that was incompatible with most of their cultural beliefs and traditions.

The Dawes Act would become the cornerstone of a new era, the era of assimilation.

What Is Assimilation?

Imagine someone made you change schools, and everyone at your new school spoke a different language than you did and only wore the color purple. To get you to fit in with everyone else, the principal of the new school made you learn this new language and took away your clothes, replacing them with unfamiliar purple clothes. In this story, you've been made to assimilate.

Assimilation is a process in which individuals or groups adopt and incorporate the customs, traditions, and ways of life of another group. This integration can happen voluntarily through cultural exchange—people can choose to assimilate to fit in with a new group of people or new surroundings. Assimilation can also happen involuntarily, or against people's will, because of outside forces. That's what happened with boarding schools.

A SOLUTION: EDUCATION

The idea of the reformers to use education as a tool to get Indigenous people to assimilate was not new. After all, the U.S. government had been funding mission schools since 1819 and was operating its own schools on reservations by the 1860s. But reformers wanted more. They viewed the very existence of reservations as a bad thing, blaming isolation from society as a reason why more Indigenous people refused to live like white people.

Like many Americans at the time, some reformers also thought it was impossible to "civilize" adult Indigenous people, and that their children only stood a chance of being integrated into white society if they were separated from their parents.

The government had its own reasons to want to educate Indigenous children. They hoped that an education would encourage Indigenous people to get jobs or to farm. Because the United States had made commitments in many treaties to provide food, housing, and health care for tribes, they looked at Indigenous self-sufficiency as a way of saving themselves money. Of course, before the government took their lands and hunting grounds, Indigenous people had been self-sufficient for thousands of years.

Educating Indigenous people would save the government money in another way—it was cheaper than going to war. Wars with tribes on the frontier had cost the government a significant amount of money, and it would cost far less to educate Indigenous children. The government believed if these children received a white education and were assimilated into white culture, it would prevent future generations from going to war.

After it was decided that education was the answer to the nation's "Indian problem," policymakers came together to decide what exactly the education of Indigenous children should involve. They decided on the following priorities:

1. Indigenous children should get enough academic instruction to learn to read, write, and speak English. Other academic subjects would be taught, but wouldn't go too far in depth, as English language mastery—and giving up their own languages—was the main goal.
2. Indigenous children should learn the value of individualism, or the prioritization of their own needs over the needs of others. This was very different from the values of most tribes, which held the well-being of a whole community or tribe above the needs of each individual person. By making children believe in individualism, policymakers hoped to give Indigenous people the desire to own their own homes and property, which would make them want to work. The schools would teach the students the kinds of jobs they wanted them to aspire to. Boys would be taught to be farmers and laborers, and girls would be taught to be domestic servants and homemakers.
3. Indigenous children would have their idea of family reshaped. Instead of thinking of family in the traditional ways of their parents and ancestors, they would be taught the white European idea of the "nuclear family," which is only made up of a mother, a father, and children. The children

would be taught that men go to work and women take care of the home.

4. Indigenous children would be taught that Christianity was better than their Indigenous religions and spiritual teachings, which white people of the time considered to be evil. Students would be forced to pray like Christians. White Americans didn't want to convert Indigenous people only because they wanted them to be saved by God, but because they thought being a Christian was the only way you could actually be considered "civilized."
5. Indigenous children would be taught how to be American citizens. They would learn American history (from the perspective of their white teachers). They would learn the virtue, or goodness, of the idea of democracy, or government by the people. They would learn to respect the flag, and feel pride in being an American, and maybe, one day, a citizen.

Once these priorities were set, it was determined that existing mission schools, or day schools and boarding schools on the reservation, could not accomplish these goals. They needed a different model, and someone to develop the schools. And for that, they'd turn to Captain Richard Henry Pratt.

CAPTAIN RICHARD HENRY PRATT

A great general has said that the only good Indian is a dead one, and that high sanction of his destruction has been an enormous factor in promoting Indian massacres. In a sense, I agree with the sentiment, but only in this: that all the Indian there is in the race should be dead. Kill the Indian in him, and save the man.

CAPTAIN RICHARD HENRY PRATT, 1892

When it came time to find an example of how this new type of school could be run, the government looked to Captain Richard Henry Pratt. His time in the army, like during the Civil War, influenced how he thought about Indigenous people, and how he wanted to educate them.

After the Red River War in 1875, hundreds of Cheyenne, Comanche, Kiowa, and Arapaho warriors surrendered to the United States at Fort Sill, in what is now Oklahoma. Pratt investigated the Indigenous men for war crimes. About 150 American Indians were accused, and 74 were brought by train to Fort Marion in St. Augustine, Florida. Pratt was put in charge of overseeing them.

Because no one had told him what to do with the

prisoners, Pratt got the idea to experiment on them, trying to figure out how to "civilize" them, or get them to act like white people. He made them wear military uniforms, cut their hair, introduced strict routines, and gave them small privileges in exchange for good behavior. He found jobs for some prisoners, doing manual labor like picking oranges and crafting souvenirs to sell. He found teachers to volunteer to teach the men to read and write.

After three years, the prisoners at Fort Marion were released, and Pratt wanted to continue his experiment. After a failed attempt to educate some of his former prisoners alongside Black men at Hampton Institute, Pratt went to Washington, D.C., to lobby for funding for his own school.

He met with many important elected officials and the secretary of war, and the government authorized Pratt to recruit 125 Indigenous students for his school and offered him space to form the school at the old army barracks in Carlisle, Pennsylvania. On October 6, 1879, the first group of students arrived.

On November 1, 1879, Carlisle Indian Industrial School formally opened, with its first class of students, who came from at least five different tribes including the Apache, Lakota, Pawnee, Cheyenne, and Kiowa. This group also included eleven former prisoners from Fort Marion who wanted to continue their education.

Some of the children were sent by their parents willingly. Other parents sent their children after being coerced or lied to. Others had their children taken to Carlisle against their will.

A member of the first class of students at Carlisle in 1880: Running Horse (Hugh).

Because of his "success" with the prisoners at Fort Marion, Pratt was incredibly stubborn in his ways. He used many of the same techniques he had used in Florida on the new students in his care. Upon arrival at Carlisle, the children underwent a drastic transformation. Stripped of their traditional clothing, they felt vulnerable and disconnected. Their Native languages were prohibited, leaving their voices silenced and their sense of identity destroyed. Their long hair was cut short to shape them into a white European ideal.

Because they were restricted to communicating solely in English, new students who only spoke their Indigenous language had an especially hard time finding their way. Stories from survivors of boarding schools often recount children crying through the night. Many of them were very young and away from their families for the first time.

Not all learning happened indoors. Boys were taught the ways of Western agriculture. They learned to sow and harvest like white farmers and to think of a plot of land as theirs alone. They were taught to plant crops favored by white Americans, which they were to sell to make a living.

Girls spent less time with textbooks and more with brooms and sewing needles. Domestic skills became their curriculum, as the government determined that a woman's place was in the home, raising children. They were educated to be housewives, mothers, and domestic servants.

Pratt wasn't quiet about how successful he believed his system was. He spoke and wrote about his efforts at great lengths. Years earlier, he had begun taking before-and-after photos of Indigenous people he "civilized," which were used as an advertisement for his technique. He continued this at Carlisle. Children would be photographed when they arrived and photographed again after they had undergone a harsh bath, haircut, and clothing change. Today, these photos provide us with a sad reminder of what students went through.

While the stories of many students and parents

reflect the bad experiences of attending the school, not every student left Carlisle feeling negatively about their education.

Lucy Black Shortnose, Anna Laura, Justine La Framboise, and Nancy Renville wearing school-issued print dresses at Carlisle in 1880.

The efforts at Carlisle were deemed a success. Quickly after the opening of Carlisle, the government announced the opening of another off-reservation boarding school, this time in Oregon. Eventually, twenty-four different off-reservation, federally run boarding schools, and even more private schools, would be created across the country using Carlisle as a blueprint.

Carlisle would go on to exist for thirty-nine years, educating upwards of 7,800 Indigenous children from more than 140 tribes. Over 1,700 Carlisle students are known to have run away, while at least 220 students are known to have died while attending the school. The site is still standing today and contains the graves of 186 Indigenous children who died while attending the school.

LET'S THINK ABOUT THIS:

1. Was it fair for the government to give land they had promised to tribes in treaties to white people through the allotment system?

2. How do you think your parents would react if someone wanted to take you to a boarding school hundreds of miles from your home?

3. How did educating Indigenous children to be "proud Americans" create differences between them and the people in their home communities?

CHAPTER 7

FOUR GENERATIONS

The "success" of the experiment at Carlisle would cause it to become the new model for the education and assimilation of Indigenous children. Although mission schools and schools for Indigenous children had existed before, Carlisle showed that children could be integrated into white American society much faster if they were separated from their families.

Starting in 1871, the United States Congress began to pass laws to force both individual Indigenous people and tribes to send their children to boarding schools. But not all parents sent their children because they had to. The reasons why a family might send their child to boarding school could be varied. Many families faced economic hardship due to the poor living conditions on reservations, which were often the result of failed treaty obligations. A parent or grandparent might have thought their child would be in a better place to succeed if they learned the skills offered by boarding schools. Not just reading and writing, but learning a trade, like how to be a carpenter or a seamstress.

Some families sent children away because they didn't have the resources to care for them. Since many tribes had suffered under decades or even a century of removal, illness, and war, money and food could be scarce, especially if a family had many children.

A studio portrait of visiting Chief Spotted Tail with his sons, then enrolled at Carlisle, 1880.

Plenty of parents refused to send their children to boarding school. Because of this resistance, many Indigenous people and tribes were coerced by government agents to send their children away.

In March 1893, Congress authorized the secretary of the interior, who oversaw the Bureau of Indian Affairs, to withhold rations, clothing, and payments for land to tribes if they didn't send their children to school. But even strict penalties couldn't get all Indigenous people to send their children away.

Efforts to get Indigenous children into school slowly succeeded. The government opened boarding schools at such an astonishing pace that by the year 1900, over twenty thousand Indigenous children were enrolled in boarding schools, both on and off the reservation. By 1925, that number would grow to over sixty thousand, or around 83 percent of Indigenous children.

WHAT KINDS OF SCHOOLS WERE AVAILABLE FOR INDIGENOUS STUDENTS?

Many denominations of Catholic and Christian churches received funding to educate Indigenous children, and the Bureau of Indian Affairs operated its own schools directly.

RESERVATION DAY SCHOOLS: *schools that Indigenous children would attend close to their home where they would leave for school in the morning and return home in the afternoon*

RESERVATION BOARDING SCHOOLS: *schools located within the bounds of a reservation, but sometimes still a far* *trip from a student's home community (during the height of boarding schools, very few people had cars, so what would now be a few hours' drive across a large reservation would have then been quite the trip)*

OFF-RESERVATION BOARDING SCHOOLS: *large schools built far away from reservations, often near an urban center. The population of students at each of these schools was around one thousand students, on average. The government built twenty-six of them in the American West between 1879 and 1902.*

What Does It Mean to Be Coerced?

"Coercion" means making someone do something they don't want to do by using force, threats, or other unfair tactics. Imagine if someone told you they would hurt you or take away something important unless you did what they wanted. That's coercion. It's like being pressured into doing something because you're scared or because you feel like you have no other choice. Coercion is not fair because it takes away someone's freedom to make their own decisions.

HOPI RESISTANCE AND THE SHERMAN INSTITUTE

While many parents and families from tribes across the country resisted sending their children to boarding school, one of the most well-documented instances of resistance occurred among the Hopi people in northern Arizona. The Hopi were not strangers to resistance. Since their first encounters with the Spanish in the 1540s, the Hopi had succeeded in keeping missionaries away from their community. Despite the presence of some Mormon missionaries, Hopi culture, languages, and traditions were still thriving when the U.S. government established the borders of the Hopi Reservation in 1882.

The official establishment of the reservation came with increased contact between the government and the Hopi. In 1887, the government built a boarding school at Keams Canyon and began to encourage families to send their children there. Just like most boarding schools, the school at Keams Canyon prohibited students from speaking their Indigenous language and practicing their traditional ways.

In addition, the school at Keams Canyon was in poor condition, overcrowded, and many children who attended the school became ill. Many Hopi parents did not want to send their children. The government and Indian agents attempted to use tactics like bribery to persuade families, but the resistance continued.

In 1890, the government sent police to enter Orayvi, the largest Hopi community at the time, and took over a hundred children to the school at Keams Canyon, which was over thirteen hours away by foot. Another roundup of Hopi children occurred four years later at Second Mesa.

Starting around that time, in 1894, the government agents for the Hopi began to report that there was a division between Hopi people who were "friendly" to the government and those who were "hostile." Almost all the Hopi wanted little to do with the government, but some were willing to accommodate Indian agents so they would leave them alone, and some fully resisted any attempts to force them to assimilate.

The government did what they could to escalate division between what they saw as two distinct groups of Hopi (a division that Hopi people reject) including calling in troops to protect the fields of the more accommodating Hopi. U.S. soldiers came onto the reservation and escalated conflict, eventually arresting nineteen Hopi resistors and taking them to prison at Alcatraz Island in the San Francisco Bay Area of California.

Reporters in San Francisco published racist stories

about the men, claiming that they were arrested only because they refused to let their children get an education. In reality, their resistance wasn't to education but to assimilation. Not only did they not want their children sent to boarding school, they also didn't want to farm land that had been individually allotted to them. They wanted to continue to farm the way that they, and their ancestors, always had.

Dr. Matthew Sakiestewa Gilbert, a Hopi scholar, cautions people against thinking of the resisting Hopi as more traditional or committed to being Hopi than their peers. In his writing, he discusses how Hopi culture values adaptation and change and celebrates Hopi migration as an important part of their history.

Those values would be put on display in 1906, when Tawaquaptewa, a Hopi leader, was forced to attend Sherman Institute. Tawaquaptewa, the leader of the more accommodating Hopi, had been a part of what was called the Orayvi split, in which the Hopi had worked to settle internal conflict through a tug-of-war. When his side had won, the other side was expelled from the village—an arrangement both sides had agreed upon.

Two months after the expulsion of the resisting Hopi, the U.S. government decided that Tawaquaptewa had acted in an un-American way, and stripped him of their recognition of his chieftainship and sent him, his family, and seventy-one Hopi children to Sherman Institute, a boarding school opened by the government in California in 1902.

Unlike most boarding school students, Tawaquaptewa was thirty-four years old. He stayed at Sherman for over three years, which was highly unusual. The government hoped that his time at the school would shape him into an influential force for sending more Hopi children away to school. He became fluent in English in less than five months and inspired the children with him to follow his lead.

While most Indigenous children were sent to boarding school without any adults from home, the Hopi children at Sherman were sent with Tawaquaptewa and other leaders. These elders acted as role models and encouraged the students to take advantage of the opportunities at school and regularly gathered Hopi students together to give them guidance and keep cultural traditions and ways of teaching, like song and dance, alive.

Hopi students who attended Sherman Institute also had the advantage of already knowing how to farm. Agricultural education was a huge part of the education offered at Sherman, and students from many tribes were completely unfamiliar with farming practices. The government wanted Indigenous people to grow crops on their allotted land, but Hopi people have some of the most advanced farming practices in the world. Many Hopi students had been farming their entire lives. While boys excelled at farming, Susie Seumptewa, another Hopi adult who was brought to Sherman, led girls in learning basket weaving, which they would have been taught at home.

The superintendent of Sherman Institute, Harwood Hall, was far more permissive of Hopi culture being shared in school than the leader of any other boarding school. His attitude, along with guidance from Tawaquaptewa and other tribal leaders, allowed the Hopi to have a different experience in boarding school than most other Indigenous children, even to use the school as a vehicle to preserve Hopi language and culture, the exact opposite purpose that the boarding school was meant to serve.

This is not to say that boarding school was a positive experience for Hopi students. Being removed from their homes and communities was still a destructive force, and students were robbed of years of the education their people could have provided them. In 1909, most of the Hopi students at Sherman Institute returned home to Orayvi. In the years that followed and with government encouragement, many of the returning students urged Hopi people to send their children away to learn about life beyond their homeland. Many would attend Sherman Institute.

LEARNING TO LIVE LIKE THE WHITE MAN

Inspired by the practices at Carlisle, the staffs at boarding schools across the United States set strict rules and schedules for Indigenous students. The rules were set to instill discipline and prepare students for assimilation into white American society. Just like at Carlisle, students at most boarding schools were forced to cut their hair, give up their traditional clothing, and wear a uniform.

Children posed for a photograph outside an unknown boarding school, ca. 1900.

Some of the things that were taught in boarding school are the same sorts of things you've learned in

Samuel High Bear and Guy (Bear Don't Scare) loading loaves onto a wheelbarrow at the Carlisle school bakery, ca. 1880.

school—reading, writing, and math. Unlike in school now, students at boarding schools began to learn a trade at an early age. Boys learned skills like farming, blacksmithing, and woodworking, while girls learned how to sew, do laundry, and cook. While this instruction was called "education" by school leaders and government officials, students were actually providing unpaid labor that reduced the cost of running the schools.

Doing this work meant that children weren't learning the skills and stories of their own people. At home, children might learn how to grow food in traditional ways, how to hunt and gather, and how to live like their elders did. Especially in the early years of boarding schools, children would have spoken their

Indigenous languages as they learned their traditional lifeways.

Students at boarding schools were required to do all their classes and schoolwork in English. Parents were often told that they couldn't use their Indigenous languages to communicate with their children while they were at school, that doing so would stunt their children's ability to learn English. Because students were often taken away to boarding school at a young age and could remain there for months or years at a time, and because they were prevented from speaking their Indigenous languages with their classmates, their ability to speak the language of their people was quickly degraded.

Losing the ability to speak the language of their families and ancestors wasn't harmful just because it made boarding school students feel distanced from their home communities. The languages we speak are the foundation of our cultures—the way that words are constructed and spoken tell us how to see the world around us, how we relate to other people, animals, and the land. When someone loses their Indigenous language, they are losing an important part of what it is to be Indigenous.

Another major goal of both government-run and church-run schools was to introduce and indoctrinate Indigenous children to Christianity. Church attendance was mandatory at many schools, and Christian faith was included in school curricula. Students were prohibited from practicing their religions or ceremonies, most of which were illegal at that time under federal law.

By removing Indigenous children from their homes and families and preventing them from speaking their languages or practicing their traditions, the U.S. government succeeded in nearly destroying one of the most important elements of Indigenous culture—the passing of knowledge from one generation to the next. Combined with the suffering that many tribes had experienced from years of disease, displacement, and war, the cutting off of traditional teaching methods had a devastating impact on Indigenous people.

NEW CULTURES, NEW CONNECTIONS

Not everything about boarding school was a negative experience. Off-reservation boarding schools created new connections between Indigenous people of different tribes, including those who may not have normally gotten along. Because students were forced to speak English, they could communicate with a broader range of their peers, laying an important foundation for intertribal connections that would allow for the beginning of the American Indian civil rights movement.

Domestic tasks, like sewing, that was taught at boarding schools allowed some Indigenous women to find work but also created new outlets for the artistic creativity that had always been an important part of Indigenous cultures.

Some Indigenous graduates of boarding schools went on to pursue further education and do important work in their fields. Many of them became some of the first Indigenous doctors, lawyers, linguists, academics, and writers.

Students at boarding schools were exposed to athletics, which would go on to become an important part of many tribal cultures and a point of pride for Indigenous people—sports like football, track and field, and baseball. Boarding school alumni became Olympians and sports stars.

Children doing calisthenics at an unknown boarding school, ca. 1900.

Here are profiles of some famous Indigenous graduates of government-run boarding schools. When reading them, it's important to remember that very few students found success in boarding schools. The accomplishments of those profiled here deserve to be celebrated, but they shouldn't distract from the suffering of most students forced to attend these schools.

ZITKÁLA-ŠÁ / GERTRUDE SIMMONS BONNIN

Zitkála-Šá (which translates to "Red Bird" in the Dakota language), or Gertrude Simmons Bonnin, was a Dakota author, musician, and activist. She was also a graduate of a religious boarding school and eventually a teacher at Carlisle Indian Industrial School. We know much about her life, including her childhood and boarding school experiences, because she wrote about them in her own words, outlining her stories in both essays and books that became popular in their time.

A citizen of the Ihaŋktoŋwaŋ Dakota Oyate, she was born on February 22, 1876, on the Yankton Dakota reservation in Dakota Territory (an area that would later become a part of the state we call South Dakota). Zitkála-Šá was raised by her Dakota mother,

Thaté Iyóhiwiŋ, after her father, a white man, abandoned the family. The youngest of her mother's five surviving children, she spent her early childhood living in a tipi and living a traditional Dakota life.

In 1884, when she was only eight years old, Quaker missionaries visited the reservation. The missionaries offered to take several Dakota children, including Zitkála-Šá, to attend White's Indiana Manual Labor Institute, hundreds of miles away from her home. While her mother was against her leaving, Zitkála-Šá was excited for an adventure, the opportunity to ride a train (which she called an "iron horse") and to eat apples. Her aunt and brother were able to convince her mother to let her leave, and so she set off with the missionaries and eight other Dakota children.

After several days of travel, they arrived at school in Indiana late at night. Since Zitkála-Šá spoke no English and had never seen electric lights or stood on wooden floors, the experience of entering the dormitory where students lived was overwhelming. She was immediately homesick and cried in the night, wishing for her mom and brother.

The next day, when she found out that her hair would be cut, she hid under a bed and was dragged kicking and screaming, then tied to a chair, as her hair was cut short. Her moccasins were traded for hard-soled shoes, and her blankets given up for a dress. As she would later write, this treatment broke her spirit. School no longer felt like an adventure but something to be survived. The teachers called her by her white name: Gertrude.

Despite everything, Gertrude took joy in learning to read and play violin and piano. After three years of being stuck in a routine she found torturous, she was allowed to return home to visit her mother during a break. Her mother tried to get her to abandon her education and stay home, but she decided to return to school.

A photograph of Zitkála-Šá, posing with her violin, in 1898.

Why did she return? We don't know. But many children who attended boarding school had trouble fitting into their home communities after leaving. Gertrude would later write that visiting home made her feel sad. She returned to White's Institute to continue her education. Her skill at both the piano and violin led the institute to hire her as a music teacher while she was still a student.

She graduated from White's in 1895 and entered the teacher-training program at Earlham College, then attended the New England Conservatory of Music to study the violin. She would later become the first Indigenous person to write an opera.

In 1897, Gertrude became an assistant teacher at the Carlisle institute. She remained on staff there for less than two years before she was forced out of her position for having views that didn't align with the institution. She would later write that it reminded her of the negative aspects of her own education and made her question the purpose of boarding schools altogether.

Following her departure from Carlisle, she began to write extensively on topics that included ending the Americanization of Indigenous students. She was widely published in popular magazines of the day, writing stories about her time growing up on the reservation and in boarding school. She also wrote about popular political issues of the time.

Her activism led to her joining the Society of American Indians and becoming an advocate for social reform and better rights for Indigenous people. She championed better education of Indigenous children, and citizenship for all Indigenous people—which was achieved in 1924. In 1926, she founded the National Council of American Indians, which still exists today. Despite her accomplishments, many people criticize Gertrude Simmons for pushing assimilation of Indigenous people into white America.

AN EXCERPT FROM *THE SCHOOL DAYS OF AN INDIAN GIRL* BY ZITKÁLA-ŠÁ

Late in the morning, my friend Judéwin gave me a terrible warning. Judéwin knew a few words of English, and she had overheard the paleface woman talk about cutting our long, heavy hair. Our mothers had taught us that only unskilled warriors who were captured had their hair shingled by the enemy. Among our people, short hair was worn by mourners, and shingled hair by cowards!

We discussed our fate some moments, and when Judéwin said, "We have to submit, because they are strong," I rebelled.

"No, I will not submit! I will struggle first!" I answered.

I watched my chance, and when no one noticed I disappeared. I crept up the stairs as quietly as I could in my squeaking shoes—my moccasins had been exchanged for shoes. Along the hall I passed, without knowing whither I was going. Turning aside to an open door, I found a large room with three white beds in it. The windows were covered with dark green curtains, which made the room very dim. Thankful that no one was there, I directed my steps toward the corner farthest from the door. On my hands and knees I crawled under the bed, and cuddled myself in the dark corner.

From my hiding place I peered out, shuddering with fear whenever I heard footsteps near by. Though in the hall loud voices were calling my name, and I knew that even Judéwin was searching for me, I did not open my mouth to answer. Then the steps were quickened and the voices became excited. The sounds came nearer and nearer. Women and girls entered the room. I held my breath, and watched them open closet doors and peep behind large trunks. Some one threw up the curtains, and the room was filled with sudden light. What caused them to stoop and look under the bed I do not know. I remember being dragged out, though I resisted by kicking and scratching wildly. In spite of myself, I was carried downstairs and tied fast in a chair.

I cried aloud, shaking my head all the while until I felt the cold blades of the scissors against my neck, and heard them gnaw off one of my thick braids. Then I lost my spirit. Since the day I was taken from my mother I had suffered extreme indignities. People had stared at me. I had been tossed about in the air like a wooden puppet. And now my long hair was shingled like a coward's! In my anguish I moaned for my mother, but no one came to comfort me. Not a soul reasoned quietly with me, as my own mother used to do; for now I was only one of many little animals driven by a herder.

JIM THORPE

James "Jim" Francis Thorpe was born in 1887 on the Sac and Fox Nation, but he also had Potawatomi, Menominee, and Kickapoo, as well as Irish and French ancestry. Thorpe is considered one of the greatest athletes of the twentieth century. However, his journey to success was not an easy one. Jim was born a twin, but his brother Charlie died when they were just eight years old during a measles outbreak at the Sac and Fox Agency School.

For a while after his brother's death, Jim left school and took to the woods, spending all day hunting and fishing. Eventually, his parents made him go back to school. But he was miserable and spent his days daydreaming, refusing to talk to other students or the teacher. Finally, he decided to leave, running the entire eighteen miles back to his family's cabin.

But his parents were committed to him receiving an education. To prevent him from running away again, they decided to send him to an off-reservation boarding school. At the age of eleven, Thorpe was put on a wagon and sent to Haskell Institute in Lawrence, Kansas. Like the other students, upon arrival he was bathed, given a uniform, and then his hair was cut. The teachers soaked his head in kerosene, a kind of gas, to kill any head lice.

Jim Thorpe in his Carlisle running uniform, ca. 1910.

Thorpe was struck by the school's harsh conditions and oppressive policies, but he discovered his passion for sports at Haskell. He excelled in track and field and was introduced to football. He made friends while playing sports and would frequently stay outside on the field after the other children had gone in.

Hundreds of miles away, Carlisle Indian Industrial School's football team, the Indians, were playing against Cornell University. The Cornell coach, Pop

Warner, was impressed by the speed of the players on the visiting team. One of the best young coaches in the country, he decided to leave his job at Cornell and move to Carlisle, to coach them and help improve the quality of their team.

In his time at Carlisle, Pop Warner led the school's football team to several victories against prestigious universities, surprising many who underestimated the abilities of Indigenous students. This success challenged the common belief at the time that Indigenous people were inferior, and it boosted the morale of the Carlisle students. The team's wins drew attention from the media and from Indigenous people across the country.

After winning a game in San Francisco, the Carlisle team boarded a train home, stopping at Indian boarding schools along the way to meet students, sign autographs, and hold football clinics. One of the schools they stopped at was Haskell, where Jim Thorpe was a student. Meeting the team left a strong impression on him.

Shortly after, Jim ran away from school after hearing that his father was ill. He walked nearly three hundred miles, but when he arrived, his father was furious. To avoid his punishment and avoid being sent back to school, Jim walked another three hundred miles to Texas, where he worked on a cattle ranch. After a year, he went back home, only to have his mother die soon after.

Losing his mom once again set Jim into a bout of loneliness and wandering. After he dropped out of a local school for white children, his father arranged for him to go to Carlisle. Shortly after he arrived, he found out that his father had died as well. He was sixteen years old. He wanted to play football, but was told he was too small, since he was only five foot five.

At nineteen, years of farmwork and a growth spurt left Jim nearly six feet tall and incredibly strong. One day, as a joke, he tried the high jump on the track field. He cleared the bar. Afterward, Jim was called to the office of Pop Warner, who also coached the track team. It turns out that Jim's jump, which he had taken with no training and in work overalls, was a new school record.

Warner immediately saw Thorpe's potential and put him on the track team. He helped Jim develop his already-remarkable athletic abilities. Even in his first season, Jim Thorpe was breaking school records and winning meets. But that wasn't enough. He still wanted to play football.

Finally, the next season, Thorpe got to play on the football team. The following summer, he played semi-professional baseball in North Carolina. At the end of the summer, instead of going back to Carlisle, he went home to Oklahoma. Pop Warner traveled all the way from Carlisle to Oklahoma to convince him to come back, but Jim refused. Finally, after meeting his former teammate Albert Exendine on the street, he agreed to go back to Carlisle.

Jim Thorpe made a name for himself in a win over Harvard University, a game he played with a sprained ankle. *The Boston Globe* wrote that he had "the heart of a lion," and even the Harvard coach said he was a "super-player." The Indians went 11-1 that season, and Thorpe was named all-American.

Thorpe's success in track at Carlisle later led to his participation in the 1912 Olympic Games, where he won gold medals in the decathlon and pentathlon. At the same Olympics, fellow Carlisle student and Diné runner Louis Tewanima won a silver medal in the 10,000-meter race.

Thorpe returned to Carlisle for one last season of football. Once again, he hadn't wanted to go back to school, but Pop Warner lured him in with the offer to play a game against the West Point football team. Carlisle would win that game, where Thorpe played against future president Dwight D. Eisenhower. That season, Thorpe scored 224 points, which was more than the total of most teams, much less players.

In 1913, Thorpe was stripped of his Olympic

medals when a newspaper report published claims that he had previously played "professional" baseball, violating the amateur status required for Olympic athletes at the time. Thorpe didn't know that the meager five dollars he had accepted for two seasons of games made him ineligible in track, because the rule had never been interpreted so strictly.

Pop Warner packed up Thorpe's medals and trophies before an investigation had even taken place, and drafted a letter from Thorpe admitting fault for the alleged rule violation. This confused the International Olympic Committee (IOC), as it was past the time where challenges to the outcome of the games were even accepted. This confusion didn't stop them from passing the medals on to the second-place finishers.

After his time at Carlisle, Thorpe went on to play six seasons of professional baseball. He also joined a football team in 1915 and would later play for six different national football teams. He became the first president of the NFL in 1920, briefly formed the NFL's only all-Indigenous team, and continued to play professional sports until he was forty-one. He died of a heart attack when he was just sixty-four.

His friends and family never stopped fighting for the return of his medals. Unfortunately, the president of the IOC, Avery Brundage, was a person who had received one of Thorpe's medals upon his disqualification. Brundage consistently denied the pleas to restore Thorpe's records and medals. Finally, in the year after Brundage left the position, the new president of the IOC granted the wishes of Thorpe's family and restored his medals, thirty years after his death.

Thorpe's achievements in sports did not erase the harsh realities of being an Indigenous student at Carlisle. He still faced the pain of being separated from his family and his culture. However, his resilience and determination allowed him to overcome these challenges and use the opportunities presented to him to excel.

Today, Jim Thorpe is remembered not just for his athletic prowess but also for his indomitable spirit and the barriers he broke. His legacy continues to inspire, serving as a testament to the strength and resilience of Indigenous people.

LET'S THINK ABOUT THIS:

1. Put yourself in the shoes of an Indigenous parent in the 1800s. Would you send your child away to boarding school? Why or why not?
2. How does what you learn in school differ from the subjects that students in boarding schools were taught?

CHAPTER 8

ABUSE, RUNAWAYS, AND RESISTANCE

While attending boarding school, Indigenous children were often prohibited from going home for long periods at a time. Like so many other parts of the boarding school experience, this was intentional.

In 1886, John B. Riley, Indian school superintendent, said that:

> *If it be admitted that education affords the true solution to the Indian problem, then it must be admitted that the boarding school is the very key to the situation. However excellent the day school may be, whatever the qualifications of the teacher, or however superior the facilities for instruction afforded by the building and school apparatus, the*

> *civilizing influence of the few short hours spent in the day school is, to a great extent, offset by the habits, scenes, and surroundings at home—if a mere place to eat and live in can be called a home. Only by complete isolation of the Indian child from his savage antecedents can he be satisfactorily educated.*

Even if their parents begged for them to come home, school officials often denied these requests. The average boarding school student was kept at school ten months a year, but many boarding school survivors recount not being able to travel home for years, often missing important milestones like funerals for loved ones.

The poor conditions at both on-reservation and off-reservation boarding schools, combined with homesickness and youthful restlessness, led to students running away—or at least attempting to—fairly often. The first few weeks of school were especially filled with students going missing and not returning to school.

After running away, students might be caught by local police or by staff of the school sent to look for them. Some students returned of their own will because they had gotten themselves into trouble or run out of food or money. If a student didn't return, the superintendent might recommend that they not be allowed to enroll anywhere else.

Running away was an important part of Indigenous resistance to boarding school, and stories of students who succeeded in making their way home were often looked to as inspiration for those wanting to make their own attempt at escape.

INDIAN BOARDING SCHOOL: THE RUNAWAYS

BY LOUISE ERDRICH

Home's the place we head for in our sleep.
Boxcars stumbling north in dreams
don't wait for us. We catch them on the run.
The rails, old lacerations that we love,
shoot parallel across the face and break
just under Turtle Mountains. Riding scars
you can't get lost. Home is the place they cross.

The lame guard strikes a match and makes the dark
less tolerant. We watch through cracks in boards
as the land starts rolling, rolling till it hurts
to be here, cold in regulation clothes.
We know the sheriff's waiting at midrun
to take us back. His car is dumb and warm.
The highway doesn't rock, it only hums
like a wing of long insults. The worn-down welts
of ancient punishments lead back and forth.

All runaways wear dresses, long green ones,
the color you would think shame was. We scrub
the sidewalks down because it's shameful work.
Our brushes cut the stone in watered arcs
and in the soak frail outlines shiver clear
a moment, things us kids pressed on the dark
face before it hardened, pale, remembering
delicate old injuries, the spines of names and leaves.

OUTING PROGRAMS

Another way that Indigenous students were mistreated at school was through outing programs. These programs were a part of the boarding school system originally created by Captain Richard Henry Pratt that spread to boarding schools created in the image of Carlisle.

Pratt had created the outing program inspired by the way he had sent prisoners out to take jobs in the community in Florida. Through the program, students would be placed with a white family during the summer months. This served three purposes: keeping students surrounded by white culture, keeping them from returning to the traditional Indigenous way of life practiced in their home communities, and providing the surrounding community with very cheap labor and courting their support of the schools.

Eventually, some students were placed into white families for an entire year and got to attend the same schools as the children in their host family. This, to Pratt, was the ideal experience, because there were no other Native children around to influence the student.

The government and school leaders said the outing program's purpose was to teach Indigenous students the importance of hard work and prepare them to live in white American society. They said it would help students learn useful skills and get ready for jobs. But instead of providing real education, the outing programs took advantage of students and made them do hard work for little to no money. The program used their labor without giving them proper education or job training, instead preparing them to be low-paid workers for the rest of their lives.

The outing programs made it even harder for Indigenous students to stay connected to their families, communities, and culture. Being cut off from their Indigenous peers hurt their sense of identity and made them feel even more isolated.

Indigenous children in outing programs were often at risk of different types of abuse, including physical, emotional, and sexual violence. Living in homes where they were seen as outsiders and treated poorly, many students faced terrible conditions. This caused long-lasting emotional and psychological harm.

ABUSE AND VIOLENCE

The hardest part about learning about the boarding schools that Indigenous children were forced to attend is learning about the history of violence, abuse, and assault that many students were subjected to.

Being forced to leave their homes, change their appearances, give up practicing their culture, and stop speaking their language was its own form of violence. Unfortunately for many boarding school survivors, those were not the worst things they experienced.

Many survivors recount abusive treatment from the staff at government and church-run boarding schools, including both sexual violence and rape. Students could be beaten or starved for speaking their language, from the moment they first arrived at school, a horrifying experience for children who were far away from home and loved ones. Strict rules about clothing, grooming, and behavior were enforced with physical violence and emotional abuse.

Beyond the abuse that happened at the schools themselves, Indigenous students were vulnerable targets for the violence of the predominantly white communities they had been transplanted into. Many boarding school survivors recount racist attacks and violence from white people they were sent to work for or interact with.

In addition to the actual violence that Indigenous students faced, the living conditions at many boarding schools were unhealthy, especially for children. Because the schools were underfunded, there could be shortages of food, dilapidated and unsafe buildings, and critical problems with disease and a lack of proper health care.

For decades, the concerns of tribal leaders and Indigenous parents about conditions for students at boarding schools went ignored. It wouldn't be until 1926, when Secretary of the Interior Hubert Work authorized a man named Lewis Meriam to study the government's treatment of Indigenous people, that most issues that students encountered would be made public.

For seven months, across twenty-three states, Meriam and his team went into the field to do research. They visited ninety-five different reservations, hospitals, and schools. While the team reported back on a variety of issues, the section of the report about the federal government's education of Indigenous children was especially upsetting. It revealed overcrowded schools and dormitories, inadequate nutrition and health care, concerning levels of tuberculosis, and a curriculum that wasn't properly preparing Indigenous children for the world.

Following the report, President Herbert Hoover requested additional funding from Congress to provide more supplies for the boarding schools, but most of the serious concerns raised in the report went ignored.

EXCERPT FROM *THE MERIAM REPORT*: "FORMAL EDUCATION OF INDIAN CHILDREN"

The outstanding deficiency is in the diet furnished the Indian children, many of whom are below normal health. The diet is deficient in quantity, quality, and variety . . . At a few, very few, schools, the farm and the dairy are sufficiently productive to be a highly important factor in raising the standard of the diet, but even at the best schools these sources do not fully meet the requirements for the health and development of the children. At the worst schools, the situation is serious in the extreme. The major diseases of the Indians are tuberculosis and trachoma. Tuberculosis unquestionably can best be combated by a preventive, curative diet and proper living conditions, and a considerable amount of evidence suggests that the same may prove true of trachoma. The great protective foods are milk and fruit and vegetables, particularly fresh green vegetables. The diet of the Indian children in boarding schools is generally notably lacking in these preventive foods . . .

Next to dietary deficiencies comes overcrowding in dormitories. The boarding schools are crowded materially beyond their capacities . . . The toilet facilities have in many cases not been increased proportionately to the increase in pupils, and they are fairly frequently not properly maintained or conveniently located. The supply of soap and towels has been inadequate . . .

The boarding schools are frankly supported in part by the labor of the students. Those above the fourth grade ordinarily work for half a day and go to school for half a day . . . However, teachers of industrial work undertaken ostensibly for education say that much of it is as a matter of fact production work for the maintenance of the school. The question may very properly be raised as to whether much of the work of Indian children in boarding schools would not be prohibited in many states by the child labor laws, notably the work in the machine laundries . . . To operate on a half-work, half-study plan makes the day very long, and the child has almost no free time and little opportunity for recreation. Not enough consideration has been given the question of whether the health of the Indian children warrants the nation in supporting the Indian boarding schools in part through the labor of these children.

GOING HOME

Even after a student was finally allowed to travel home, their time away at boarding school often left Indigenous boarding school survivors to feel out of place. They may have gone years without speaking their language, so communication with their families and community could be very difficult. They had been taught that white culture was better than their Indigenous ways, so they could have a lot of internalized racism against their own people.

Most often, going home caused a bit of an identity crisis for boarding school survivors. They had been taught how to get along in white society, how to farm and eat and pray like white people. None of these skills served them at home. Many returning

A Thanksgiving Day play at an unknown boarding school, ca. 1900.

students struggled to find work and suffered from depression and low self-esteem. Many had strained relationships with their parents, who could feel guilty or resentful of their children for no longer fitting into their community.

WHAT IS INTERNALIZED RACISM?

Internalized racism is a concept that can be tricky to understand. It's when someone starts to believe the negative things others say about their own race or culture. Imagine if someone told you over and over that you can't be good at math because of your skin color, and after a while, you start believing it. That's internalized racism, and it's harmful because it hurts people's self-esteem and because it can cause them to look at other people of their race and believe harmful stereotypes about them.

One way that we can try to empathize with students who survived boarding school is by reading the stories and poems of boarding school survivors and their descendants. Here are two examples.

EVERYTHING YOU NEED TO KNOW IN LIFE YOU'LL LEARN AT BOARDING SCHOOL

BY LINDA LEGARDE GROVER

Speak English. Forget the language of your grandparents. It is dead. Forget their teachings. They are ignorant and unGodly. Cleanliness is next to Godliness. Indians are not clean. We will teach you to be clean. You will never amount to anything. Stand in line. You will practice proper hygiene. This is a toothbrush. Hang it on the hook next to the others. Do not allow the bristles to touch. This spreads the disease that you bring to school from your families. Make your bed with mitered corners. A bed not properly made will be torn apart. Start over. The boarding school feeds and clothes you. Remember and be grateful. Say grace before meals. In English. Don't cry. Crying never solved anything. Write home once every month. In English. Tell your mother that you are doing very well. You'll never amount to anything. Answer when the teacher addresses you. In English. We do not recommend visits to your family. If you visit your family in the summer, report to the matron's office immediately upon your return. You will be allowed into the dormitory after you have been sanitized and de-loused. Busy hands are happy hands. Keep yourself occupied. You'll never amount to anything. Books are our friends. Reading is your key to the world. In English. Forget the language of your grandparents. It is dead. We forbid you to speak it. If you are heard speaking it you will kneel on a navy bean for one hour. Don't cry. Crying never solved anything. We will ask if you have learned your lesson. You will answer. In English. Spare the rod and spoil the child. We will not spare the rod. We will cut your hair. We will shame you. We will lock you in the basement. Learn from that. Remember and be grateful. Speak English. You'll never amount to anything.

EXCERPT FROM "DITCHED" BY JIM NORTHRUP

A young one on the little guys' side of the dormitory would begin quietly crying. Maybe he was crying because he was lonely and homesick, maybe he had been assaulted by a big guy. Whatever the reason, the boys on either side of him would tell him to be quiet. When the little guy wouldn't quit crying, the ones next to him would be reminded how homesick they were and start crying also. We could hear the wave of crying start at one end of the dormitory and come traveling down until the boy next to you was crying and you were sobbing also. I suspect all the boys were crying because it was the only thing we could do. After a night like that, we all got up in the morning and pretended that it didn't happen.

LET'S THINK ABOUT THIS:

1. If you were forced to go to a boarding school, would you take a chance and run away? Why or why not?
2. Why would people think that it was acceptable to make Indigenous children work while we had laws that prevented white children from working?

CHAPTER 9

SHIFTING TIDES

As the twentieth century began, many Indigenous children were still enrolled in boarding school. But changes were on the horizon. Legislation in 1917 prohibited schools and government agents from coercing parents into sending their children to school. By the 1920s, new regulations prohibited the enrollment of children younger than fourteen in most boarding schools.

In 1924, Congress passed the Indian Citizenship Act, finally acknowledging Indigenous people as citizens of the United States and giving states the ability to grant voting rights to them. One side effect of this was transferring the responsibility of educating Indigenous children to public schools run by states and local governments. Before Indigenous people were citizens, they didn't have the right to a public education. After becoming citizens, Indigenous children had the right to attend public schools, and local schools became the default option for young students especially.

In 1933, when Franklin Delano Roosevelt became president, he appointed a man named John Collier as his commissioner on Indian Affairs. Collier, who was the executive director of the American Indian Defense Association, had been deeply influenced by his experiences living at the Taos Pueblo in New Mexico. He recognized the inherent value of Indigenous cultures and the severe impact federal policies like boarding schools had on their communities. His work had helped inspire the 1928 Meriam Report, and now he was going to lead the charge in implementing its recommendations.

Collier aimed to reverse the damage done by the long-term policy of assimilation and land theft through what would come to be known as the Indian New Deal. In 1933, he worked with Congress to pass the Pueblo Relief Act, which sought to compensate the Pueblo tribes for land lost to squatters. He then championed the passage of the 1934 Johnson–O'Malley Act, which authorized federal contracts with state and local governments for educational, health, and social services for tribes. But his biggest project was ahead of him.

THE REORGANIZATION ERA

The most important piece of policy of this new era was the Indian Reorganization Act (IRA). The IRA sought to allow tribal communities to govern themselves—but only in the ways that the American government found acceptable. The IRA also aimed to protect Indigenous lands and let tribes buy back land that had been sold after allotment, but it made compromises about land ownership by allowing some Indigenous people who had land to keep it instead of forcing them to give it to a tribe.

The IRA allowed tribes to create their own governments, but they still had to follow federal rules. This meant that tribal constitutions needed federal approval and had to be approved by a majority of adult tribal members during a special election called by the secretary of the interior.

The IRA also included some assistance for Indigenous economies. It let tribes create businesses, set up sustainable farming and grazing programs on reservations, created a $10 million fund for start-up loans for Indigenous businesses, and set aside $250,000 for vocational and trade schools.

After the IRA was passed, each tribe had to vote on whether they wanted to accept the new law. Collier thought most tribes would like self-government under the IRA, but many Indigenous people didn't support it. Almost a third of the tribes that voted on the IRA rejected it. Only 38,000 out of 97,000 eligible tribal members voted, which meant some tribes had the IRA applied to them without support from their citizens.

Different tribes had different reasons for rejecting the IRA. Some Indigenous people thought it was a good start but didn't go far enough in fixing the problems caused by the government during years of displacement and genocide.

Other tribes felt that the IRA forced them to adopt a style of government that was too similar to the U.S. government, which they weren't used to. It was a sort of "one-size-fits-all" approach, but because each tribe was different and had their own culture and traditions, it didn't work for everyone.

In 1938, Onöndowa'ga:' (O-non-dowa-gah) journalist Alice Lee Jemison said: "The Wheeler–Howard Act [another name for the IRA] provides only one form of government for the Indian and that is communal or cooperative form of living. John Collier said he was going to give the Indian self-government. If he was going to give us self-government, he would let us set up a form of government we wanted to live under. He would give us the right to continue to live under our old tribal customs if we wanted to."

Beyond the IRA, Collier also helped pass the Indian Arts and Crafts Act of 1935, which protected the authenticity of products produced by citizens of tribal nations. This was important, because selling these products was, and remains, an important source of revenue for many Indigenous people and tribal communities.

On the education front, Collier worked to close many boarding schools, encouraging investment in schools on reservations and practical job training programs. In 1934, Collier closed ten boarding schools. Boarding school enrollments dropped from 22,000 to 17,000, and his 1935 budget funded only 13,000 students. Under his tenure, the enrollment at reservation day schools sharply increased, and he encouraged the teaching of culturally sensitive education methods that sought to improve student performance.

Just like many well-intentioned white people, Collier often thought he knew was best for Indigenous people without really asking them what they wanted. This made him unpopular in many places. In some communities, like the Navajo Nation, Collier's policies did great harm. The government had come up with equations for how many livestock they thought tribes should have, and they decided that the Diné had too many. They used this as an excuse to kill nearly half of the sheep that the Diné kept. Collier remained the commissioner of Indian Affairs until 1945.

Many of the stated goals and promises of the Indian Reorganization Act failed for a variety of reasons. Tribes were hesitant to trust the same government that had spent a century trying to kill them, take their land, and take their children. Many departments within the federal government were still deeply against the concept of Indigenous sovereignty. And beyond all that, more and more Indigenous people were already assimilating into white American society, moving to cities, and leaving their homelands in search of prosperity.

What Is Self-Determination?

Tribal self-determination is the concept that tribes have the right to govern themselves. Let's break it down into some important parts:

"Sovereignty" is a fancy word that means having the power to rule over yourself. For Native American tribes, this means they can make their own laws and decisions without needing permission from the U.S. government. It's like how states can make their own rules, but for tribes, it's even more special because it's about their unique cultures and histories.

A tribal government is the group of people who

run a Native American tribe. Just like the president and Congress run the country, tribal governments have leaders who make decisions for their community. They might decide on things like education, health care, and how to use their land.

The trust relationship is the connection between the U.S. government and Native American tribes. The government has promised to protect the tribes' lands and rights. In return, tribes sometimes give up some of their land or follow some federal laws. Think of it like a special agreement or promise to help each other out.

Tribal self-determination is important because it allows tribes to manage their own affairs and it allows citizens of those tribes to elect leadership to represent their interests and protect their sovereignty. It respects their rights as the original people of this land and helps them build strong, healthy communities.

THE TERMINATION ERA

Starting in the 1940s, the federal government once again took a turn in its approach to tribes: It attempted to terminate the special, unique trust relationship between tribal governments and the federal government. This was yet another attempt to get Indigenous people to assimilate.

From June 1940 to September 1950, major laws were passed that allowed states to have some control over tribes and reservations. In 1949, the Hoover Commission suggested that Native Americans should be included more in white society. The 1952 House report that investigated the Bureau of Indian Affairs described the idea of ending tribes' special status as a cheap and harmless option.

House Concurrent Resolution 108 was passed on August 1, 1953. It stated that Congress believed the U.S. government should immediately end the supervision of tribes and treat Indigenous people like any other non-native U.S. citizens. This meant ending reservations and tribal sovereignty and forcing Indigenous people to attempt to fit into white American society. This resolution was passed at the same time as Public Law 280, which gave states control over civil and criminal matters involving Indigenous people in Alaska, California, Minnesota, Wisconsin, Oregon, and Nebraska, where many Indigenous people live.

The government said that these changes were supposed to help Indigenous people become self-sufficient, but they often led to loss and hardship.

This process involved stripping them of their federal recognition, which meant they lost access to important services and benefits guaranteed to them in treaties. For example, when a tribe was terminated, they could no longer receive funds for education, health care, and other services that the government had provided. The loss of these benefits had a devastating effect on many tribes.

One of the most famous cases was the termination of the Menominee (Meh-nom-eh-nee) tribe in Wisconsin. In 1954, the government decided to terminate the Menominee's status as a tribe. This decision meant that they lost their protected lands and rights as a tribe. Although they received a small amount of money from the government, it did not replace the loss of their land or culture. Many Menominee people struggled to adjust to their new situation, as they had relied on their tribal relationships and communal living for many years. The tribe struggled financially and was forced to sell large portions of their land to a private developer. After a lot of hard work, the tribe was recognized by the federal government once again in 1973.

The impact of termination policy was devastating for many Indigenous people. During this era, more than a hundred tribes were terminated (over forty-four in California alone,) affecting approximately

1.3 million acres of tribal land. This policy led to significant economic and social problems among Indigenous communities, many of which continue to this day. Without federal recognition, many tribes lost their land and resources. Many Indigenous people were forced to move to cities, where they struggled with poverty, discrimination, and a loss of their cultural identity.

The termination era is a somber period in U.S. history, reflecting yet another time when the government prioritized assimilation over the preservation of Indigenous cultures. It is a reminder of the significant struggles and injustices that Indigenous people have faced.

Today, the effects of the termination era still linger, with many Indigenous communities working tirelessly to reclaim their rights, regain their lands, and preserve their cultures.

RELOCATION

One major event of the termination era was the passage of the 1956 Indian Relocation Act, which encouraged the widespread relocation of Indigenous people from their reservations to cities like Chicago, Denver, and Los Angeles. The government told Indigenous people that moving to these cities would help them get better jobs and higher education. The relocation program often targeted younger tribal members, hoping that this younger generation would be more receptive to the change. The government offered incentives for relocating, such as assistance with moving costs and job training—but these incentives often fell short of the actual needs of the Indigenous people who were relocated, leaving many to struggle with the transition.

Once in the cities, many Native Americans were faced with a grim reality. The jobs they were promised were often low paying, and the living conditions were poor. Tribal members also faced discrimination and prejudice, further hindering their ability to succeed and thrive in these urban settings. Policies like redlining, the establishment of boundaries where

The graduates of Bureau of Indian Affairs Intermountain Indian School in Utah prepare to leave for jobs in Los Angeles, 1956.

certain people couldn't buy homes because of their race or religion, prohibited Indigenous people from buying homes in white-dominated areas, which were often safer and had better schools.

The separation from their tribal communities and traditions led to a loss of cultural identity for many. Indigenous culture is intimately tied to ancestral lands. When people moved away from their homelands, many found it difficult to maintain their traditions and pass their cultures on to the next generation. For all these reasons, many Indigenous people who joined relocation programs quickly returned home.

For those who stayed, the effects of relocation weren't all negative, though. In the cities, many Indigenous people found a new sense of community. They came together, forming "urban Indian" communities and organizations that sought to provide support and maintain cultural traditions. Some even used their urban experiences to bring about positive change in their home communities.

However, despite these pockets of resilience and adaptability, the overall impact of relocation was incredibly harmful. It further eroded tribal sovereignty by lowering reservation populations and further disrupted Indigenous cultures that had already been impacted by centuries of genocide, war, displacement, and disease.

LET'S THINK ABOUT THIS:

1. How did the termination and relocation era continue the pattern of the government telling Indigenous people how to live?
2. Why might it be difficult for people to move away from their reservations and go to the city?

ADOPTED OUT: LILA'S STORY

Rapid City, South Dakota, 1965: Lila lay in on her bunk bed, missing her grandmother. She had been taken from her when she was just seven years old. She had spent years at an orphanage before being adopted by the Millers. Although she had been with them for four years, Lila still felt a deep sense of loss. Every night, she'd gaze out her bedroom window, where the city lights replaced the stars, longing for the warmth of her siblings in the bed next to her.

Lila remembered the times she spent with her family on the reservation. Her grandma would gather her and her siblings around a crackling fire, under a blanket of stars, and tell them stories like that of Iktomi, the trickster spider, and funny stories about the trouble Grandma had gotten into as a youngster in boarding school.

But in her new home, Lila felt those connections fading. Her adopted family couldn't understand the emptiness she felt or why she mourned the loss of a life they thought they had saved her from. They didn't know about the taste of her grandmother's soup or the feeling of freedom she felt under the million stars she could see at home.

Early on, Lila tried to share stories of her home—the animals she'd find and dogs she'd chase, the days spent running in the dirt with her cousins, the comfortable chaos of family gatherings—but her words seemed to vanish into the air, unheard as her new mom and dad would quickly change the subject. In school, when teachers asked about her background, Lila felt a sharp sting of embarrassment. She began to see herself through her classmates' eyes, and what she saw made her heart sink. The reservation, her culture, the essence of who she was—it all seemed to dwindle in the shadow of her new life.

One evening, after a particularly hard day at school, Lila lay on her bed, tears soaking her pillow. She felt torn between two worlds but belonging to neither.

It was then that Lila decided to push away her

Lakota roots altogether, convinced that fitting in meant erasing the parts of her that were different. She buried her memories of the reservation, of her grandparents, and of the traditions that shaped her. Lila forced herself to speak, act, and think as she believed her adopted family and friends wanted her to.

After years of trying her hardest, she graduated high school. Lila had grown up to embody the image of success she always thought she wanted. She excelled in school, landed a good job, and even started a family of her own with a nice man whose family lived near hers. But with every achievement, the whispers of her past got louder, calling her back to the parts of herself she had tried to leave behind.

A void remained inside her, an emptiness that nothing could fill. It was a longing for connection, for understanding, for the culture and family ties she had suppressed for so long. Lila realized that in trying to adopt a new identity, she hadn't just distanced herself from her roots; she had lost a part of her soul.

Lila had never told her children about her heritage, her family, or the reservation she hailed from. But as she watched them grow, she recognized a familiar ache in their eyes—the same yearning to understand who they were and where they came from. Lila knew then that denying her heritage didn't just erase her own identity; it robbed her children of theirs as well.

She desperately wanted to go back home but was filled with fear. Would anyone remember her? Would they see her as too different, or be embarrassed that she no longer remembered any of her language? Would they accept her children as their family too?

One day, she hoped she'd be brave enough to try.

CHAPTER 10

GONE BUT NOT FORGOTTEN

Without our relatives, we cease to exist. So with Native people, part of our wealth is in our family, it's in who we are connected to.

TERRI YELLOWHAMMER, JUDGE, CITIZEN OF THE STANDING ROCK SIOUX TRIBE WITH HERITAGE IN THE WHITE EARTH NATION

Lila's story was not unique. Unfortunately, the decline of the boarding school system didn't mean an end to the cultural genocide of Indigenous peoples by the U.S. government. As boarding schools were closed, the government thought of a new way to break up Indigenous communities—giving up Indigenous children for adoption, often against the will of their parents.

In 1958, the Bureau of Indian Affairs established the Indian Adoption Project. The program aimed to place Indigenous children away from their home communities, frequently into non-Indigenous families that lived far away from the child's family of origin. The BIA used a massive media campaign to encourage white families to adopt Indigenous children, often lying and saying that the children were orphans, that they were unwanted, and that they needed saving.

The program was enormously impactful: During the program's years of operation, from 1958 to 1967, between 25 and 35 percent of tribally enrolled children were stolen from their families. Among this group, over 85 percent were adopted into non-Indigenous families. The program was another tool of assimilation, done under the guise of helping the children. But just like the boarding school system, it had many negative consequences.

The Indian Adoption Project functioned by actively encouraging and facilitating the removal of Indigenous children from their families and communities in sixteen Western states. Social workers, often without clear explanation to a child's family, or even against their will, would place Indigenous children into foster care or adoption systems without consideration for their cultural heritage or well-being. Mothers were threatened with penalties if they didn't give their children up for adoption, or they were deceived into signing away their parental rights.

These actions were justified by a belief that

integration into white, middle-class families was in the best interest of the children, offering them better opportunities than their own communities could. However, this process stripped the children of their cultural identity and heritage, as they were placed with families who typically had little to no understanding or respect for the child's Indigenous culture, languages, or traditions.

Many Indigenous people and governments opposed the program, but their voices were drowned out. Children were often placed in homes far from their tribes and were not taught about their heritage—even worse, many were lied to about their parents, the reasons why they were adopted, and even where they came from.

These adoptions were intentionally "closed," meaning that the child who was adopted had no contact with their birth family or relatives. Children were often placed far away from their home communities, to ensure that any connection they had to their culture was eliminated, causing many Indigenous adoptees to grow up feeling disconnected from their culture and struggling with their identity. This practice is known as "forced assimilation."

The Indian Adoption Project was a way for the government to continue the mission of boarding schools—to destroy Indigenous culture. And unlike the boarding schools, adoption was less visible, so it was harder for anyone concerned with the well-being of Indigenous children to call attention to the problem.

Though the project was active only until 1968, the practice of forced assimilation continued well into the 1970s, resulting in thousands of Indigenous children being taken from their families and communities. Many were never able to reconnect with their culture or their birth families. The lasting impact of these policies and practices has been referred to as "historical trauma," affecting generations of Indigenous people who have been disconnected from their roots and identities.

What Is a Family of Origin?

"Family of origin" means the family that a person was born into. For example, if a child is adopted, their family of origin would include their birth parents and any siblings they might have had before being adopted. Even if a child is adopted into a new family, they still have their family of origin, which is where they originally came from. It's like the roots of a tree—even if the tree is planted somewhere new, it still has its original roots where it began growing. Understanding and respecting a child's family of origin is important because it helps them know where they come from and can be a part of who they are.

LET'S THINK ABOUT THIS:

1. Why would the government want to separate Indigenous children from their families and home communities?

2. Do you think it would be better for Indigenous children to be adopted by Indigenous or non-Indigenous families? Why?

AUNTIE BINESHI GOES TO WASHINGTON

Standing on the chilly sidewalk in 1972 Minneapolis, Minnesota, a ten-year-old Ojibwe boy named James took in the city skyline. He had spent the morning wandering up and down his block, despite the dropping temperatures. He was eagerly awaiting the arrival of one of the most vivid figures in these streets, his auntie Bineshi, whom he admired more than anyone else. She was younger than his mom, and so much more exciting. She had gone off to college in Chicago, and she was finally coming home.

Bineshi wasn't just a family member to James; she was a hero straight from the stories his grandfather whispered to him at night. She was a part of the

American Indian Movement (AIM), a group of people who stood bravely for the rights of Native people like him. James knew very little about politics, but he knew that his auntie was a warrior, fighting for the rights of their people to have a better life. His mom and grandma disagreed, often calling her and her friends troublemakers. They worried too much.

One late-autumn day, when the trees were already almost completely bare, Auntie Bineshi sat James down at the kitchen table. It was littered with papers. The faint aroma of sage lingered in the air as she slurped down her coffee. Whatever she was working on, she'd been doing it all night.

"I've got to travel to Washington with my friends," she said, her voice growing louder. "We're going to make a stand, a really big one. It's time they heard our voices, James."

His eyes widened. This task seemed like something big and important, the kind of thing he increasingly heard the adults around him speak of with a mixture of respect and frustration. Watching Auntie Bineshi prepare for this journey felt exciting. "Can I come too?" he asked. Before his mom could chime in, his auntie reminded him that he had to go to school.

Weeks later, James watched out the window with pride as Auntie Bineshi opened the door of the van that would carry her away. She was fearless. One day he would be like that, he swore. She loaded in her signs and jumped into the back seat, her two long black braids trailing behind her.

As James waved goodbye from the frosty window, he had no way to understand the true importance of where his aunt was headed—to take part in what AIM called "the Trail of Broken Treaties." Hundreds of Indigenous activists, coming from both cities and reservations across the United States, were planning to go to Washington, D.C., to demand advances in the civil rights of their people.

Word spread quickly that the caravan had begun to occupy the Bureau of Indian Affairs. For seven days, the activists took over the building, bringing attention to their platform and negotiating with the BIA and even federal leaders. Teachers at his school said terrible things about what was happening, but James knew to ignore what his aunt had taught him was racism against his people.

James and his whole family waited for word from his auntie, desperate to know more about what was happening and if she was all right. His mother pretended not to worry, while her pacing in the kitchen of their apartment told another story.

Finally, they got a call. His auntie was getting

ready to board a bus back home. Her work had made the whole country notice. James swelled with pride. He suddenly felt a foot taller. Auntie Bineshi and her friends had planted a seed of courage within him, and he was ready to take on the world.

CHAPTER 11

SELF-DETERMINATION AND THE CIVIL RIGHTS ERA

The 1960s and 1970s were a time of powerful social movements and calls for change in many communities. By the late 1960s, Indigenous people also started to organize and demand their rights. They wanted to maintain their cultural identities and protect their lands. The Pan-Indian civil rights movement began to form. Indigenous activists sought to protect Indigenous lands, uphold treaties, and improve the conditions of tribal people across the nation.

THE AMERICAN INDIAN MOVEMENT

One important organization during this time was the American Indian Movement (AIM). AIM was established in Minneapolis in 1968 to help Indigenous people in the city work together to address problems related to poverty, discrimination, and the loss of their rights. Like so many other groups fighting for their civil rights in this era, AIM held protests and demonstrations to bring attention to their struggles and fight for justice.

A photograph of the Longest Walk, a five-month march from San Francisco, CA, to Washington, D.C., in 1978 in protest of legislation that would revoke treaties, limit Indigenous rights, and greatly decrease access to social services.

Despite facing backlash and violence from government authorities, AIM successfully brought attention to issues such as tribal sovereignty, land rights, education, and health care. They also fought against forced assimilation policies, racism, and discrimination.

In addition to their activism, AIM began to open what they called "survival schools." These schools emerged as a response to the inadequate education provided by government-run boarding schools. They aimed to provide culturally relevant education that celebrated Indigenous history, language, and values.

The importance of cultural revitalization was also recognized in the passage of the Indian Self-Determination and Education Assistance Act of 1975, which allowed tribes to take control of their own educational systems. This led to the establishment of tribally controlled colleges and universities, where Indigenous students could learn about their heritage while pursuing higher education.

The efforts of AIM and other activists led to other key legislative changes, including the American Indian Religious Freedom Act of 1978, which protected the rights of Native Americans to practice their traditional religions, ceremonies, and cultural activities, which had been illegal up until then.

As a result of efforts of organizations like AIM, the state and federal governments began to change their approach. In the 1970s, new policies focused on self-determination for Native American tribes. This meant that tribes had the right to govern themselves and make decisions about their future. The government started to recognize the importance of tribal sovereignty and provided funding to help tribes restore their governments and cultural practices.

THE OCCUPATION OF ALCATRAZ

One of the first major actions by Indigenous activists in the 1960s was the occupation of Alcatraz, the infamous former prison in the middle of San Francisco Bay. The occupation began on November 20, 1969,

A group of men fish off the Alcatraz dock during the occupation of Alcatraz Island, 1969.

by eighty-nine Indigenous activists from several tribes, most of whom were students. Initially, media coverage seemed empathetic to the message of the activists, who had constructed tipis on the island, issued demands, and painted signs declaring *Native Pride* and *Red Power.* Several celebrities visited the island to attract more coverage and speak with the students.

The activists published their demands in *The Movement* newspaper, in January 1970:

> *To the Great White Father and All His People:*
>
> *We, the native Americans, re-claim the land known as Alcatraz Island in the name of all American Indians by right of discovery.*
>
> *We wish to be fair and honorable in our dealings with the Caucasian inhabitants of this land, and hereby offer the following treaty:*
>
> *We will purchase said Alcatraz Island for twenty-four dollars (24) in glass beads and red cloth, a precedent set by the white man's purchase of a similar island about 300 years ago. We know that $24 in trade goods for these 16 acres is more than was paid when Manhattan Island was sold, but we know that land values have risen over the years. Our offer of $1.24 per acre is greater than the 47 cents per acre the white men are now paying the California Indians for their land.*
>
> *We will give to the inhabitants of this island a*

portion of that land for their own to be held in trust by the American Indian Affairs and by the bureau of Caucasian Affairs to hold in perpetuity—for as long as the sun shall rise and the rivers go down to the sea. We will further guide the inhabitants in the proper way of living. We will offer them our religion, our education, our life-ways, in order to help them achieve our level of civilization and thus raise them and all their white brothers up from their savage and unhappy state. We offer this treaty in good faith and wish to be fair and honorable in our dealings with all white men.

We feel that this so-called Alcatraz Island is more than suitable for an Indian reservation, as determined by the white man's own standards. By this we mean that this place resembles most Indian reservations in that:

1. *It is isolated from modern facilities, and without adequate means of transportation.*
2. *It has no fresh running water.*
3. *It has inadequate sanitation facilities.*
4. *There are no oil or mineral rights.*
5. *There is no industry and so unemployment is very great.*
6. *There are no health care facilities.*
7. *The soil is rocky and non-productive and the land does not support game.*
8. *There are no educational facilities.*

9. *The population has always exceeded the land base.*
10. *The population has always been held as prisoners and kept dependent upon others.*

Further, it would be fitting and symbolic that ships from all over the world, entering the Golden Gate, would first see Indian land, and thus be reminded of the true history of this nation. This tiny island would be a symbol of the great lands once ruled by free and noble Indians.

What use will we make of this land?

Since the San Francisco Indian Center burned down, there is no place for Indians to assemble and carry on tribal life here in the white man's city. Therefore, we plan to develop on this island several Indian institutions:

1. *A CENTER FOR NATIVE AMERICAN STUDIES will be developed which will educate them to the skills and knowledge relevant to improve the lives and spirits of all Indian peoples. Attached to this center will be traveling universities, managed by Indians, which will go to the Indian Reservations, learning those necessary and relevant materials now about.*
2. *AN AMERICAN INDIAN SPIRITUAL CENTER which will practice our ancient*

tribal religious and sacred healing ceremonies. Our cultural arts will be featured and our young people trained in music, dance, and healing rituals.

3. *AN INDIAN CENTER OF ECOLOGY which will train and support our young people in scientific research and practice to restore our lands and waters to their pure and natural state. We will work to de-pollute the air and water of the Bay Area. We will seek to restore fish and animal life to the area and to revitalize sea life which has been threatened by the white man's way. We will set up facilities to desalt sea water for human benefit.*
4. *A GREAT INDIAN TRAINING SCHOOL will be developed to teach our people how to make a living in the world, improve our standard of living, and to end hunger and unemployment among all our people. This training school will include a center for Indian arts and crafts, and an Indian restaurant serving native foods, which will restore Indian culinary arts. This center will display Indian arts and offer Indian foods to the public, so that all may know of the beauty and spirit of the traditional INDIAN ways.*

Some of the present buildings will be taken over to develop an AMERICAN INDIAN MUSEUM, which will depict our native food and other cultural contributions we have given to the world. Another part of the museum will present some of the things the white man has given to the Indians in return for the land and life he took: disease, alcohol, poverty and cultural decimation (as symbolized by old tin cans, barbed wire, rubber tires, plastic containers, etc.). Part of this museum will remain a dungeon to symbolize both those Indian captives who were incarcerated for challenging white authority, and those who were imprisoned on reservations. The museum will show the noble and the tragic events of Indian history, including the broken treaties, the documentary of the Trail of Tears, the Massacre of Wounded Knee, as well as the victory over Yellow Hair Custer and his army.

In the name of all Indians, therefore, we re-claim this island for our Indian nations, for all these reasons. We feel this claim is just and proper, and that this land should rightfully be granted to us for as long as the rivers shall run and the sun shall shine.

Signed,
Indians of all Tribes
November 1969
San Francisco, California

Unfortunately, these demands were never met. For months, the federal government basically ignored the occupation, attempting to wait the activists out. This plan worked, as activists slowly began to leave. They had families and homes to return to, and life on the island was difficult. Finally, in June 1971, President Richard Nixon issued an order to end the nineteen-month occupation and escort the last group of activists off the island.

Even though the activist's stated demands were not met, the occupation of Alcatraz brought attention to rising Indigenous activism. Activism began to spread across the country, motivating Indigenous people, especially youth, to act and stand up for their rights.

TAKEOVER OF THE BUREAU OF INDIAN AFFAIRS

In November 1972, following the occupation of Alcatraz, activists from eight organizations, including the American Indian Movement, the National Indian Youth Council, and Indians of All Tribes, took over the Bureau of Indian Affairs (BIA) building in Washington, D.C.

The takeover happened after a nationwide protest called "the Trail of Broken Treaties." Indigenous people from all over the country traveled to Washington, D.C., to bring attention to the problems their communities were facing. They brought a list of twenty demands, including better housing, education, and respect for their treaties. When government officials wouldn't meet with them, protesters entered the BIA building and stayed there for about a week. They wanted to send a strong message that Indigenous people deserved to be treated fairly.

The government was surprised and upset by the takeover, but it showed how serious Indigenous people were about fighting for their sovereignty. It was a powerful moment in history that helped bring more awareness and respect to injustices committed against tribes and their citizens. While there was initial backlash against the protesters for causing

A poster for the Trail of Broken Treaties cross-country protest in 1972. Participants advocated for better housing, education, and employment for Indigenous Americans.

trouble, their list of demands would go on to be the center of the Indigenous rights agenda for decades.

THE NEED FOR CHANGE

Another major issue that activists were concerned about was the continued removal of Indigenous children from their families. As awareness of this injustice grew, activists, tribal leaders, and community members began to advocate for change. They argued that Native children should have the right to grow up within their own cultures, surrounded by their families and communities.

In response to coercive adoption practices, activists and tribal communities intensified their efforts in the 1970s. They sought to make visible the grim realities of cultural erasure and identity disruption that these policies facilitated. Through organized protests, strategic advocacy, and harnessing the media, they aimed to bring national attention to the plight of Indigenous children.

By the mid-1970s, the push for reform had started to gain traction. One important moment was the testimony before the Senate on abuses in the adoption process and its impact on Indigenous communities.

Heart-wrenching personal stories and concrete data presented by tribes, social workers, and Indigenous activists highlighted the urgency of the issue. It was this collective action that catalyzed legislative change, ultimately leading to the drafting of the Indian Child Welfare Act (ICWA), which was aimed at keeping Native American children with Native families and within their tribal culture.

THE CREATION OF THE INDIAN CHILD WELFARE ACT

ICWA marked a big change from previous approaches to adopting out Indigenous children, setting federal standards for their removal from families and placement in foster or adoptive homes. The law granted tribal governments control in child welfare cases, acknowledging the sovereignty of Native tribes and their inherent right to care for their children based on their own laws, customs, and practices. The enactment of ICWA was a significant victory for activists who had long fought for the end of abusive and assimilationist policies.

The Indian Child Welfare Act established guidelines and procedures to ensure that Indigenous children were placed in culturally appropriate settings whenever possible. Key provisions of ICWA include:

1. **TRIBAL JURISDICTION**: ICWA recognizes the tribal sovereignty and tribal authority over child welfare matters within their communities. Tribes have the right to intervene in child custody proceedings involving Indigenous children and to determine the best interests of the child based on tribal customs and traditions.
2. **PLACEMENT PREFERENCES**: The law prioritizes placement of Indigenous children with extended family members, members of their tribe, or other Indigenous families whenever possible. This helps to maintain familial and cultural connections for Indigenous children who are unable to remain with their birth parents.
3. **CULTURAL CONSIDERATIONS**: ICWA requires that courts and child welfare agencies take into account the cultural and familial ties of Indigenous children when making placement decisions. This includes consideration of the child's tribal affiliation, language, religion, and traditions.
4. **NOTIFICATION AND CONSULTATION**: Before an Indigenous child can be removed from their home or placed in foster care or adoption, ICWA mandates that tribes be notified and given the opportunity

to participate in the proceedings. This ensures that tribes have a voice in decisions affecting their children and families.

IMPACT OF ICWA

The Indian Child Welfare Act has had a very large impact on tribal communities, helping to preserve Indigenous cultures, protect children, and strengthen families. By prioritizing the placement of children with relatives and within their own communities, ICWA has reduced the trauma of removal and helped to maintain cultural connections for generations to come.

However, despite its importance, ICWA has faced legal challenges and implementation issues over the years. Some critics argue that the law interferes with the rights of non-Native parents and imposes undue burdens on state child welfare systems. These challenges highlight the ongoing need for education and advocacy to ensure that ICWA is upheld and enforced effectively.

Despite all the successes of ICWA, Native American children are still placed in foster care at a higher rate than any other ethnic group.

COMING BACK INTO THE LIGHT

Because of the work of activists and tribal leaders, in 1978, Congress passed the American Indian Religious Freedom Act, a federal law that protects the rights of Native Americans to practice their traditional religions and ceremonies.

The law guarantees Native Americans the following rights:

1. **FREEDOM TO PRACTICE**: the right to believe, express, and practice traditional religions
2. **ACCESS TO SACRED SITES**: the right to access sacred sites
3. **USE AND POSSESSION OF SACRED OBJECTS**: the right to use and possess sacred objects
4. **FREEDOM TO WORSHIP**: the right to worship through traditional rites and ceremonies

Despite Indigenous religions and traditions being illegal for so long, they did not go away. Like oppressed people everywhere, Indigenous people had pushed their practices underground, sometimes maintained by just a few trusted practitioners.

The passage of the American Indian Religious

Freedom Act allowed a vibrant and diverse array of traditions to come back into the light. This, combined with the growing embracement of Pan-Indian culture, led to the growth of the powwow community, where Indigenous people still gather to sing, drum, dance, and spend time with family.

Across the country, the door began to open for Indigenous people to publicly reclaim their pride in their cultures, speak their languages, practice traditional foodways, and restore traditional kinship systems.

Artists and poets like Suzan Shown Harjo used their creativity to talk about the pain that Indigenous people had experienced during centuries of colonization:

CHILDREN IN THE MEADOWS AND WETLANDS

BY SUZAN SHOWN HARJO

There are children in the meadows and wetlands
Native children ran there to hide
When teachers pulled and butchered their hair
When teachers stole their medicine bags
When teachers collected their moccasins
When teachers dressed them in strange clothes
When teachers beat them with boards and belts
When teachers starved them for being bad Indians
The children ran to the meadows and wetlands

There are children in the meadows and wetlands
Hostages who were taken to Haskell
Who never saw their families again
Who never saw nine or eleven or tomorrow
Who didn't make it home for summer vacations
Who couldn't stop whooping and coughing
Who couldn't learn English fast enough
Who wouldn't fall to their knees often enough
They ran 'til they fell in the meadows and wetlands

There are children in the meadows and wetlands
Hostages who were taken to Chilocco
Where they ran from teachers' fists and boots
Where they ran from bounty-hunters' cages
Where they ran from high collars and hard shoes
Where they ran from lye soap in their mouths
Where they ran from day and night
Where they ran until wolves outran them
Their teeth are in the meadows and wetlands

There are children in the meadows and wetlands
Hostages who were taken to Carlisle
Who got to build the school buildings
Who got Christian burials without coffins
Who got a mass grave with their friends
Who got plowed under for a football field

Who got embedded in concrete for the stadium
Who got to be the practice site for the Washington Redskins
Because they ran to the meadows and wetlands

There are children in the meadows and wetlands
Native children ran there to hide
You can see their clothes in museums
You can see their pipe bags at the opera
You can see bands marching on their hallowed ground
You can see mascots dancing over their dead bodies
You can imagine their hair long and beautiful again
Safe from teachers and scissors at last
These children in the meadows and wetlands

LET'S THINK ABOUT THIS:

1. Why do you think it was important to activists to demand religious and cultural freedom?
2. What freedoms are important to you?

CHAPTER 12

WHAT DOES IT MEAN TO SURVIVE?

The trauma of shame, fear and anger has passed from one generation to the next, and manifests itself in the rampant alcoholism, drug abuse, and domestic violence that plague Indian country. Many of our people live lives of unrelenting tragedy as Indian families suffer the ruin of lives by alcoholism, suicides made of shame and despair, and violent death at the hands of one another.

FORMER UNITED STATES ASSISTANT SECRETARY FOR INDIAN AFFAIRS KEVIN GOVER (PAWNEE)

The harm of genocide, war, disease, boarding schools, and removal could not be instantly overcome by the movement for Indigenous rights and Native pride. These traumas have had serious and lasting effects on Indigenous peoples and communities. The attempted destruction of

Indigenous languages, traditions, and family connections led to hurt that many people still feel today. We call this legacy of pain "historical trauma."

Historical trauma happens when bad things from the past still cause pain to people today. Imagine if your great-grandparents went through something very difficult, like being forced to leave their home. Even though it didn't happen to you, you might still feel sad or have problems because of it. This is because the hurt and sadness can be passed down, like an old story, but one that makes people feel bad instead of happy.

Historical trauma affects the health of Indigenous peoples in serious ways, not just adults but also children and teenagers. We call this passing on of trauma "intergenerational trauma." Because so many generations of Indigenous people were forcibly removed from their families, people can lack role models for healthy parenting.

Intergenerational trauma is like a heavy backpack filled with sadness and anger that can get handed down through families, from parents to children and so on. Think about it as an invisible kind of injury that isn't about scraped knees or broken bones but about feelings and experiences that hurt inside. It doesn't feel good to know your people were treated so horribly.

For example, Indigenous kids had their ancestors go through very hard times, like being removed from their land or being placed in boarding school. Those feelings of fear or sadness can stick around, even though they didn't happen to the kids directly. Sometimes, these feelings can make it hard for the next generations to feel happy or successful. It's like a shadow from the past that follows people around, and it's the job of friends, families, and communities to understand this shadow, talk about it, and bring more light into each other's lives.

But the impacts go beyond hurt and sadness—the legacy of violence affects the health of Indigenous people. On top of historic and intergenerational trauma, many Indigenous people live in poverty, which at its root is caused by the theft of land and resources by the government and its continuous failure to live up to treaty obligations. Being poor makes it difficult to access healthy, traditional foods, and that can lead to chronic illnesses like diabetes and heart disease. The emotional toll can be even more devastating, leading to mental health challenges, addiction to drugs and alcohol, and high rates of suicide. All these challenges create a cycle that makes it harder for Indigenous communities to be healthy. This shows how important it is to create health programs and services that understand their history and help them today.

ALL OF THIS FOR WHAT?

The boarding school system was a horrific failure in its promises to Indigenous parents, students, and communities. For all the trauma that they caused, the programs also left Indigenous people poorly educated, with most boarding school students failing to ever graduate. This legacy is still evident in Indigenous communities today, where a very small minority of students ever graduate from college.

Tim Giago, an Oglala Lakota former student of the boarding schools and founder of the first independently owned Native American newspaper in the U.S., said in 2006:

> *I speak not for myself alone, but for the thousands of Indian men and women who struggled for years to find themselves. Many succeeded, but many failed. We went out into the world away from the Mission boarding schools lost and confused.* If we were not Indian, what were we? *We soon realized that in the real world, we were different. In South Dakota we*

were not accepted in the world we had been trained to become a part of. With the lack of acceptance came the terrible feelings of rejection that became the focal point of so many of our lives. Our self-esteem had been obliterated. Many of us were actually ashamed to be Indian.

KAMLOOPS AND CALLS FOR INVESTIGATION

For a long time, many people in the United States and Canada had never heard of boarding schools for Indigenous children (called "residential schools" in Canada). But in 2021, something very sad was discovered at the Kamloops Indian Residential School in British Columbia, Canada, that brought the issue of boarding schools to the news across the world. A survey of the former school's apple orchard revealed the unmarked graves of 215 Indigenous children who had gone to the school.

For non-Indigenous people, this was a shocking and heartbreaking discovery, because it showed how horribly these children had been treated. For Indigenous people, this was evidence of the harm that so many of our families know too well.

The discovery of the unmarked graves brought

the story of boarding schools to a larger audience than ever before. Across Canada, communities began to talk about the pain caused by residential schools and the possibility of more bodies on the properties of other former schools.

In the United States, the discovery prompted newly appointed Secretary of the Interior Deb Haaland (who had also been the first Indigenous secretary of the interior, which oversees the Bureau of Indian Affairs) to announce a task force to investigate the treatment of children in schools once operated by the BIA.

The BIA report, which was released in 2024, concluded a three-year investigation that saw, for the first time, the federal government accepting responsibility for its role in creating the system, which included more than four hundred schools across thirty-seven states. It revealed that the government had spent the equivalent of over $23 billion in today's money on the boarding school system between 1871 and 1969.

The report increased the official count of boarding schools in the United States from 408 to 417, across thirty-seven states. The number includes twenty-two schools in Alaska and seven in Hawaii. Worst of all, the report concluded that at least 973 American Indian, Alaska Native, and Native Hawaiian children died while attending government-operated boarding schools. The BIA states that the actual number of children who died while attending boarding schools is likely greater, due to policies that often sent sick children home to their families to avoid their deaths being counted in official reports.

In its 2024 report, the BIA concludes that the federal government must take actual action to address the harm done. They recommend that the minimum that the government must do is take the same amount of money they spent on boarding schools—$23 billion—and invest it in the economic development and well-being of tribal nations.

LET'S THINK ABOUT THIS:

1. What feelings come up when you hear how negative of an impact colonization, boarding schools, and cruel government policies have had on Indigenous people?
2. Ask your family: Were there major hardships that your ancestors experienced? Does it have an impact on you today?

A DAY IN THE LIFE OF ODE

Onamia, Minnesota, 2025: Ode woke up to the sunlight streaming through his bedroom window, lighting up the art projects he had scattered around his room. As he rubbed the sleep from his eyes, he smiled, remembering that today was a special day at his school. He quickly dressed in his favorite shirt, which was printed with traditional Anishinaabe floral designs. He grabbed a hearty breakfast of manoomin (wild rice) and ode'iminan (strawberries), which his gookomis (his grandmother) had prepared for him.

After breakfast, Ode made his way to school, the mitigoog (trees) surrounding his grandma's house alive with the sounds of birds singing and leaves rustling in the gentle breeze. He loved walking to school, where he could greet his friends with a cheerful "Boozhoo!" (Hello!) in Anishinaabe as they approached the brightly painted building that served as their school.

Throughout the day, Ode learned about Anishinaabe history and culture in his Indigenous language, which he'd been speaking since he was a baby. His favorite class was art, where they were working on creating beadwork patterns, a skill passed down through generations in his family. Maybe one day his work would lie as smooth and flat as his mom's.

In the cafeteria, students snacked on venison and squash, both of which were grown right there on the reservation. After lunch, his class ventured outside for a chilly afternoon storytelling session, where elders from the community shared tales of the Anishinaabe people and the trickster Wenabozhoo. The snow was almost melted, so soon these storytelling sessions would turn into an hour for the hard work of spring. Ode enjoyed the last of the stories, listening intently, his imagination taking flight.

As the school day came to an end, Ode joined his friends at drum group practice. The drum echoed loudly in the gym and made him feel alive. He lost himself in the moment and almost stuck his drumstick in his eye. Afterward, as he walked down the long road toward home, he could still feel the beat and hear his teacher singing backup.

That night, as he sat down with his grandma, mom, dad, and sister for dinner, they shared stories of their day, and he taught his parents a few new words he'd learned. This always filled his grandma with joy and annoyed his sister, which was a plus.

As Ode drifted off to sleep that night, he practiced repeating the stories he'd heard from his elders that day, preparing for the day that he'd repeat them to the next generation.

THE TRUTH, TODAY

WHAT IS LIFE LIKE FOR INDIGENOUS CHILDREN TODAY?

Despite all the challenges that Indigenous people have been through during more than five centuries of colonization and genocide, we are still here. Across the United States, there are over 574 recognized tribes and 326 reservations. Over 3.7 million people identified as American Indian or Indigenous in the 2020 Census.

Indigenous people today live both on reservations and off them, with more than half of tribal citizens now living in cities and suburbs. On the reservation, the Bureau of Indian Education (BIE) still operates 183 schools. Unlike the BIE schools of the past, these schools are mostly run under the leadership of the tribes themselves. The BIE also operates four off-reservation boarding schools, all of which were originally founded in the nineteenth century but operate very differently than they did a hundred years ago.

The biggest difference between schools during the boarding school era and today is that parents have agency—they get to choose what schools are right for their children, not government agents or school leaders.

Other exciting new options have emerged for Indigenous children, like schools that specifically focus on Indigenous culture and unique ways to help Indigenous children learn.

LANGUAGE & CULTURAL REVITALIZATION

In the boarding school system, great effort was made to get children to speak English and forget their Indigenous languages. Students could be beaten, deprived of food, and isolated for speaking the languages they grew up with.

Despite that, most Indigenous languages did not disappear. But severe damage was done. Across Turtle Island, the name many Indigenous people use to refer to North America prior to colonization, many tribes came close to losing the remaining speakers of their language.

Some tribes, especially the larger ones, were able to maintain many speakers. But over the years, between boarding schools, adoption, and intergenerational trauma, most Indigenous people missed the opportunity to learn their people's language while growing up.

Yet there are bright spots emerging today. As tribes are able to build their economies, many are focusing on cultural revitalization—the mission of bringing their culture back to its full vibrancy. And language is an important part of that.

Building on the work that was done by decades of Indigenous activists and educators, many tribes today are offering lessons in their languages to citizens, even teaching children in what's called "immersion classrooms," where only Indigenous languages are spoken, and classes like math and science are taught using culturally relevant activities. Students might learn fractions while also learning how to make maple syrup.

Even at schools and colleges off reservations, Indigenous languages are being taught. While many of these languages are still considered "endangered," or at risk of being lost, there is finally hope for restoration.

Many Indigenous language scholars look to people from around the world, like the Māori in New Zealand and Indigenous Hawaiians, for guidance in restoring languages that faced so much harm.

CAN COUNTRIES REPAIR THE HARM THEY CAUSE?

In some countries where colonial governments did horrible things to Indigenous people, like Canada, governments and tribal people have come together to go through a process sometimes called "truth and reconciliation." This might take place in the halls of government or in tribal buildings. In these processes, tribal leadership, witnesses, historical experts, and government officials come together to recount and create a public record of wrongs done by the government.

Canada's truth and reconciliation process is a way for the country to address and understand the injustices and mistreatment that Indigenous peoples have faced. This process began after it was revealed that many Indigenous children were taken from their families and placed in residential schools. Just like boarding schools in the United States, these schools were also run by the government and churches, and their purpose was to force Indigenous children to assimilate into European-Canadian culture, which often meant they were not allowed to speak their native languages or practice their traditions.

For many years, students at these residential schools suffered from neglect, abuse, and poor living conditions. As more people learned about these wrongdoings, Canadians realized that it was crucial to acknowledge the past and work toward healing and making things right. This led to the establishment of the Truth and Reconciliation Commission (TRC) in 2008.

The TRC was designed to record and share the truth about what happened at residential schools. It collected statements from survivors, visited communities, and held events where people could speak about their experiences. The TRC aimed to educate all Canadians about the history and lasting impacts of residential schools.

In 2015, the TRC published a final report with ninety-four "Calls to Action." These are recommendations for how Canada can move forward in the journey of reconciliation. They cover various areas, including education, health, justice, and child welfare, and they ask both the government and Canadians to work together to repair relationships and create a better future.

Reconciliation means working to restore friendly relations and make amends for past wrongs. For Canada, this involves recognizing the importance of

Indigenous cultures, honoring treaties, and supporting the well-being of Indigenous communities.

Although the truth and reconciliation process has been far from perfect and has been criticized by some Indigenous Canadians, it provides one way of opening the door to repair.

WHAT'S NEXT?

Does America need a truth and reconciliation process? This is not what most Indigenous scholars and activists are asking for. When you ask what the United States can do to repair the harm done by policies of child removal, most Indigenous people will tell you that the government must first stop causing harm. This means honoring tribal sovereignty, fulfilling treaty and economic obligations, and listening to Indigenous activists working to protect the land.

Many Indigenous activists are now also calling for Land Back—a movement to restore the control of Indigenous lands to Indigenous people. This includes federal lands, lands taken through allotment, and land granted to tribes in treaties. In some places, this has already started to happen in small ways.

Some Indigenous scholars call for a return to the

treaty-making process. This would allow the government and tribes to reenter negotiations and for tribes to determine what could be done to repair harm.

Indigenous people know that justice cannot exist until we are in right relationship with the land. Our children can't be truly safe or cared for until the land that is their birthright is also cared for.

LET'S THINK ABOUT THIS:

1. What tribes live in the area where you live?
2. What Indigenous languages are spoken in the area around where you live?
3. What do you think could be done to repair the harm that the U.S. government has done to Indigenous people?

AUTHOR'S NOTE

I first learned about boarding schools from my grandma Emma, who attended Flandreau Indian School in Flandreau, South Dakota. Her boarding school experience left her with immense trauma. Even into her nineties, she would cry out in her sleep, remembering how she was treated by the staff at Flandreau.

As I researched boarding schools in college and at my first museum job, she told me her own stories. I was also learning our language, Anishinaabemowin, my grandma's first language, which the staff at Flandreau had attempted to beat out of her. Although she has moved into the next world, her stories are forever in my heart, reminding me of the importance of telling the truth about the history of this country.

In one story, my grandma recounted a specific memory, one that I think of often. Children at her school were denied food if they spoke their Native language. Because she and other children knew how hard it was to miss a meal, they would smuggle bread from dinner, which they squished into tight balls and hid in their pockets. At night, when hungry children would cry, the smugglers would give them their balls of bread to soothe their empty stomachs.

Nookomis, this book is for you.

A COMPREHENSIVE LIST OF BOARDING SCHOOLS

526 schools
125 schools open today that were or are considered Indian boarding schools
38 states

THE TOP FIVE STATES WITH THE MOST BOARDING SCHOOLS WERE:

Oklahoma (98)
Arizona (59)
New Mexico (52)
South Dakota (35)
Alaska (30)

FOURTEEN DENOMINATIONS WERE REPRESENTED

Anglican
Baptist
Catholic
Dutch Reformed
Episcopal
Evangelical
Jesuit
Mennonite
Methodist
Presbyterian
Protestant
Quaker
Seventh-day Adventist
Unitarian

ALABAMA (2)

Asbury Manual Labor School and Mission
Wills Town Mission School

ALASKA (30)

Anvik Mission (Christ Church)
Bethel Regional High School and Dormitory
Copper Valley Boarding School
Covenant High School
Douglas Island Friends Mission School (Mayflower School)
Eklutna Industrial School
First Mission House (Bethel Indian School)
Fort Wrangell Tlingit Industrial (Wrangell Training Academy)
Friends High School (Kotzebue Friends School)
Galena Interior Learning Academy

Haines Mission and House
Holy Cross Boarding School (Kosoreffsky)
Jesse Lee Home for Children
Kanakanak Hospital, Orphanage, and School
Kodiak Aleutian Regional High School
Mt. Edgecumbe Boarding School (Mt. Edgecumbe High School)
Nenana Student Living Center
Nunapitsinghak Moravian Children's Home
Our Lady of Lourdes Orphanage and Mission
Russian Bishop's House
Seward Sanitarium
Sitka Industrial Training School (Sheldon Jackson Institute)
St. Mark's Episcopal Mission
St. Mary Mission School
St. Pius X Mission
Victory High School (Victory Bible School)
White Mountain Boarding School
William E. Beltz Boarding School (Nome-Beltz Middle High School)
Woody Island Mission and Orphanage (Longwood School)
Wrangell Institute

ARIZONA (59)

Blue Canyon Boarding School (Western Navajo Boarding School)
Chinle Boarding School
Colorado River Boarding School
Dennehotso Boarding School
Dilcon Boarding School (Dilcon Community School)
East Fork Lutheran Mission School
Fort Apache Boarding School (White Mountain/Whiteriver)
Fort Defiance Boarding School (Navajo Industrial School; Navajo Training School)
Fort Mojave Industrial School (Herbert Welsh Institute)
Ganado Navajo Presbyterian Mission (Kirkwook Memorial Training School)
Greasewood Boarding School (Greasewood Springs Community School)
Greyhills Academy High School
Havasupai Boarding and Day School
Holbrook Indian School (Seventh Day Adventist Indian School)
Hunters Point Indian School
Jeehdeez'a Academy
Kaibeto Indian School
Kayenta Indian School (Kayenta Community School)
Keams Canyon Boarding School (Moquis Industrial; Hopi Training; Keams Canyon Elementary School)
Kinlichee Indian School (Kinlichee Lichi'i Olta')
Klagetoh Boarding and Day School
Leupp Boarding and Day School (Leupp Schools)
Low Mountain
Lukachukai Boarding and Day School (Lukachukai Community School)
Many Farms Community School
Many Farms High School
Marsh Pass School (Kayenta Sanatorium)

Navajo Mountain School (NaaTsis'Aan Community School)
Nazlini Boarding School (Nazlini Community School)
New Jerusalem Mission Boarding School (Globe)
Phoenix Indian School (Peel Institute)
Pima Boarding School (Sacaton Central School)
Pine Springs Boarding School
Pinon Boarding School (Pinon Community School)
Red Rock Boarding School (Red Rock Day School)
Rice Station Boarding and Day School
Rock Point Boarding School (Tsé Nitsaa Deez'áhí Diné Bi'ólta'; Rock Point Community School)
Rocky Ridge Boarding School
Rough Rock Community
San Carlos Boarding and Day School
Santa Rosa Boarding School
Santa Rosa Ranch Boarding School (Santa Rosa Ranch School)
Seba Dalkai Boarding School
Shonto Boarding School (Shonto Preparatory School)
Southwest Indian School
Steamboat Canyon Boarding School
St. John's Indian School
St. Michael Indian Industrial School (Chi'hootsoi Biolta'; St. Michael Indian School)
St. Peter Indian Mission School (Gila River)
Teec Nos Pos Boarding School (Teec Nos Pos Community)
Theodore Roosevelt Indian Boarding School (Fort Apache/Theodore Roosevelt School)
Tolani Lake School
Tolchaco Mission School (Navaho Mission Boarding)
Toyei Boarding School
Truxton Canyon School (Valentine Indian School)
Tuba City Boarding School (Westen Navajo Indian School)
Tucson Indian Training School (Tucson Presbyterian School)
Walapai Indian School (Hualapai)
Wide Ruins Boarding School (Kinteel Olta'; Wide Ruins Community School)

ARKANSAS (1)

Dwight Presbyterian Mission School

CALIFORNIA (13)

Anaheim Boarding School
Fort Bidwell Indian Boarding School
Fort Yuma Indian Boarding School
Greenville Indian Industrial Boarding School
Hoopa Valley Boarding School
Middletown Training School
North Fork Presbyterian Mission
Perris Indian School
Round Valley Indian School
Sherman Institute (Sherman Indian High School)
St. Anthony's Industrial School for Indians
St. Boniface Indian School
St. Turibius Mission Boarding and Day School

COLORADO (5)

Fort Lewis Indian Boarding School (Fort Lewis College)
Good Shepherd Industrial School (E.M. Byers Home for Boys)
Grand Junction Indian School (Teller Institute)
Southern Ute Boarding School (Ignacio Boarding School)
Ute Mountain Boarding School

FLORIDA (1)

St. Augustine School for Apache Children at Fort Marion (Fort Marion; Castillo de San Marcos)

GEORGIA (2)

High Tower Mission School (Etowah Mission School; Etonee School)
Spring Place Mission School

HAWAII (29)

Ahuimanu College (Rev. R. A. Walsh School; St. Louis School)
Chief's Children's School (Royal School)
English Sisters' School
Hilo Boarding School
Industrial and Reformatory School (Waialee, Waialua)
Industrial and Reformatory School for Girls (Maunawili/Kawailoa Training Schools for Girls; Olomana School; Hawaii Youth Correctional Facility)
Kamehameha Schools (Bishop School)
Ka'ū Seminary
Kawaiaha'o Female Seminary
Kohala Female Seminary (Hawaiian Girls' School)
Koloa Family School
Makawao Female Seminary (East Maui Female Seminary; Mauna 'Olu Female Seminary; Mount Holyoke Seminary of the Hawaiian Islands)
Makiki Family School
Mauna Loa Forestry Camp School
Miss Bingham's School
Molokai Forestry Camp School
Mr. W. Gulick's School
Mrs. L G Lyon's School
Lahainaluna Seminary (Lahainaluna High School)
O'ahu Charity School (Town Free School; Mililani Girls' School)
Punahou School (Oahu College at Kapunahou; School for Missionaries' Children at Punahou)
Rev. D. Dole's School
Rev. G. Mason's School (St. Alban's School)
Sisters of the Sacred Hearts' School
St. Alban's College
St. Andrew's Priory School
Territorial Normal and Training School (Teacher's College, University of Hawaii)
Waialua Female Seminary (Rev. O.H. Gulick's School; Hale'iwa; Central Female Seminary; Waialua English School)
Wailuku Female Seminary (Maui Female Seminary)

IDAHO (7)

Fort Hall Boarding School (Lincoln Creek)
Fort Lapwai Training School

Good Shepherd Boarding School (Episcopal Mission)
Lemhi Boarding School
Mary Immaculate School at the Mission of the Sacred Heart of DeSmet
Nez Perce Boarding School
St. Joseph's Mission School

ILLINOIS (2)

Homewood Boarding School (Jubilee College)
St. Mary's Training School for Boys (Feehanville School; Maryville Academy)

INDIANA (2)

St. Joseph's Indian Normal School
White's Manual Labor Institute, Indiana

IOWA (4)

Sac & Fox Boarding School
Toledo Industrial Boarding (Toledo Sanatorium; Sac & Fox Indian Boarding School; Sac & Fox Sanatorium)
White's Manual Labor Institute, Iowa (Iowa Boys Training School; Iowa Girls Training School)
Winnebago Mission School (Yellow River School)

KANSAS (13)

American Indian Institute (Roe Indian Institute)
Halstead Mennonite Mission Boarding School
Haskell Indian Industrial Training School (Haskell Indian Nations University)
Iowa and Sac and Fox Indian Mission School
Iowa and Sac and Fox of Missouri Boarding School (White Cloud Indian Industrial Boarding School)
Kaw Methodist Mission School
Kickapoo Boarding School
Osage Manual Labor School for Boys and Osage School for Girls
Pottawatomie Boarding School (Hoyt Boarding School)
Pottawatomie Mission Boarding School (Topeka Mission Labor School)
Shawnee Methodist Indian Mission (Shawnee Methodist Mission and Indian Manual Labor School)
St. Mary Mission and School
Shields Female Academy

KENTUCKY (1)

Choctaw Indian Academy

MICHIGAN (8)

Assinins Orphanage
Baraga Chippewa Boarding and Day School (Holy Name)
Catholic Otchippewa Boarding School
Holy Childhood of Jesus School (New L'Arbre Croche Mission School)
Holy Family Orphanage (Marquette Holy Family)
Mackinac Mission School (Michilimackic School)
Mount Pleasant Indian Industrial Boarding School
New Mission House (Grove Hill Seminary)

MINNESOTA (23)

Ah-Gwah-Ching Sanatorium (Consolidated Chippewa Sanatorium)
Bena Boarding School
Cass Lake Boarding School
Catholic Industrial School of Minnesota
Covenant of our Lady of the Lake (Graceville School)
Cross Lake Indian Residential School (Ponemah Boarding School)
Leech Lake Indian Boarding School
Mission of Our Lady of the Sacred Heart Indian Industrial School
Morris Industrial School for Indians (University of Minnesota Morris)
Nett Lake Boarding and Day School
Pine Point Boarding and Day School
Pipestone Indian School
Red Lake Boarding and Day School
St. Benedict's Academy at Saint Joseph (College at St. Benedict)
St. Benedict's at White Earth (White Earth Boarding School)
St. John's Indian Industrial School (St. John's University)
St. Mary's Mission Boarding and Day School (Red Lake Mission Boarding School)
St. Paul's Industrial School (Clontarf Industrial School)
St. Rose/St. Francis Xavier School and Holy Child Academy
St. Theodore's Mission School
Vermillion Lake Indian School
White Earth Boarding School
Wild Rice River Boarding and Day School

MISSISSIPPI (7)

Bethel Mission School
Charity Hall Mission School
Choctaw Central Indian School (Choctaw Central Middle and High School)
Eliot School
Emmaus Mission School
Martyn Mission School
Mayhew School

MISSOURI (2)

Harmony Mission School (Osage Indian School)
St. Regis Seminary (Florissant Mission School; St. Stanislaus Seminary)

MONTANA (20)

Blackfeet Agency Boarding and Day School (Blackfeet Dormitory)
Crow Agency Boarding School
Crow Mission School
Flathead Agency Boarding and Day School
Fort Belknap Boarding and Day School
Fort Peck Agency Boarding School (Poplar Creek Boarding School)
Fort Shaw Government Industrial Indian School
Holy Family Mission and School (Holy Family Industrial School)
Montana Industrial School for Indians (Bond's Mission School)
Northern Cheyenne Tribal School
Pryor Creek Boarding School
St. Charles Mission School

St. Ignatius Mission and School (Academy of the Holy Family for Young Ladies; Flathead Agency Boy's Boarding; Flathead Agency Girls' Boarding)
St. Labre Indian Mission Boarding School (St. Labre at Busby; St. Labre Indian School)
St. Paul Mission and Boarding School
St. Peter Mission School
St. Xavier Mission School (Pretty Eagle Catholic Academy)
Tongue River Boarding School (Busby Indian School)
Willow Creek Boarding School
Wolf Point Mission Boarding and Day School

NEBRASKA (10)

Genoa Indian Industrial School
Iowa Industrial School (Orphans Industrial Home)
Omaha Indian School
Omaha Mission Boarding
Otoe Missouria Indian Mission School
Santee Industrial School
Santee Normal Training School
Silver Ridge Seminary
St. Augustine Mission School
Winnebago Boarding School

NEVADA (4)

Fort McDermitt Indian Boarding School
Pyramid Lake Boarding and Day School
Stewart Indian Boarding School (Carson Industrial School)
Western Shoshone Indian School

NEW MEXICO (52)

Alamo Navajo School (Alamo Navajo School Board, Inc.)
Albuquerque Indian School (Indian Pueblo Training School; Fiske Institute)
Baca Boarding and Day School
Beclabito Boarding School (Beclabito Day School)
Canoncito School (To'Hajiilee Community School)
Charles H. Burke Indian School (Fort Wingate Indian School; Wingate High School)
Cheechilgeetho Boarding School (Chichiltah-Jones Ranch Community School)
Chuska Boarding School (Ch'ooshgai Community School)
Coyote Canyon Boarding and Day School
Crownpoint Boarding School (T'iis Ts'ozi Bi'Olta')
Crystal Boarding School
Dzilth-Na-O-Dith-Hle Community School
Huerfano Dormitory (Hanáádli Community School/Dormitory, Inc.)
Institute of American Indian Arts
Iyanbito Boarding School
Jicarilla Apache Boarding School (Jicarilla Southern Mountain Sanatorium; Jicarilla Dormitory)
Laguna Sanatorium
Lake Valley Navajo School

Manuelito Navajo Childrens Home
Mariano Lake Boarding School (Mariano Lake Community School)
Menaul School
Mescalero Boarding School (Mescalero Apache School)
Mexican Springs Boarding School
Naschitti Boarding School (Naschitti Elementary School)
Nava Boarding and Day School
Navajo Farmington Methodist Mission School (Navajo Preparatory School)
Navajo Farmington Presbyterian Mission School
Navajo Jewett Mission (Liberty Indians Boarding School)
Nenahnezad Boarding School (Nenahnezad Community School)
Pinedale Boarding School
Pine Hill Boarding School
Pueblo Pintado Boarding School (Pueblo Pintado Community School)
Ramah Navajo High School
Ramona Indian School
Rehoboth Mission School (Rehobeth Christian School)
San Juan Training School
Sanostee Boarding School (Sanostee Day School)
Santa Fe Indian School (Dawes Institute)
Shiprock Indian Boarding School
Sisters of Loretto School (Bernalillo Boarding School)
Southwestern Indian Polytechnic Institute
St. Catherine Indian School
Standing Rock Boarding School (Tse'ii'ahi' Community School)
Thoreau Boarding School
Toadlena Boarding School (To'haali' Community School)
Tohatchi Boarding and Day School
Torreon Community School (Na'Neelzhiin Ji'Olta)
Twin Lakes Boarding School (Twin Lakes Elementary School)
White Horse Lake Boarding School
Zuni Boarding School (Zuni Sanatorium; Blackrock Sanatorium School)

NEW YORK (7)

Convent of Our Lady of Mercy School (Indian Girls Industrial School at Hogansburg)
Friends Boarding School for Indian Children (Tunasassa Indian Boarding School)
Seneca Mission and School (Buffalo Creek Mission)
Thomas Indian School (Gowanda School; Thomas Asylum)
Tonawanda Mission School
Tuscarora Indian School (Mount Hope Indian School)
Western New York Home for Homeless and Dependent Children (Randolph Children's Home)

NORTH CAROLINA (4)

Cherokee Boarding School (Eastern Cherokee Training School)
Judson College
Trinity College Industrial Indian Boarding School (Duke University)
Valley Towns Baptist Mission School

NORTH DAKOTA (18)

Bismarck Indian School (Mandan Indian School)
C. L. Halls' Congregational Mission Home School—Elbowoods (Fort Berthold Indian Mission School)
Fort Berthold Agency Boarding School (Elbowoods Community School)
Fort Stevenson Boarding School
Fort Totten Indian Industrial School (Whipple Institute)
Fort Totten Indian School
Fort Yates Government School (St. Peter Catholic Mission School)
Little Flower Mission School
Maddock Agricultural and Training School (Benson County Agricultural and Training School; Maddock Public School)
Our Lady of Sorrows
Sacred Heart Mission School (Fort Berthold Indian Mission School)
St. Ann's Indian Mission School (Ojibwa Indian School)
St. Edwards Mission Boarding School
St. Mary's Indian Industrial School (Turtle Mountain)
St. Michael's Manual Labor School
St. Michael's Mission School (Our Lady of Sorrows Chapel and School; Seven Dolors Mission)
Standing Rock Agency Boarding School (Standing Rock Community School)
Wahpeton Indian School (Circle of Nations)

OHIO (1)

Shawnee Friends Mission and School

OKLAHOMA (98)

Absentee Shawnee Boarding School
Arapaho Manual Labor and Boarding School
Armstrong Academy
Asbury Manual Labor School
Bloomfield Female Academy
Burney Institute (Lebanon Orphan School; Chickasaw Orphan Home and Manual Labor School)
Carter Seminary
Cache Creek Mission School
Cantonment Boarding School (Mennonite Boarding School)
Cherokee Colored Boarding School
Cherokee Female Seminary—Park Hill
Cherokee Male Seminary
Cherokee Orphan Training School
Cheyenne Manual Labor and Boarding School
Chickasaw Children's Village
Chickasaw National Academy
Chickasaw Manual Labor Academy (Harley Academy)
Chilocco Indian Agricultural School (Haworth Institute)
Chishoktak Boarding and Day School
Choctaw and Chickasaw Sanitorium School
Chuahla Female Seminary
Creek Orphan Home
Colbert Institute
Collins Institute

Coweta Boarding School
Darlington Mission School (Mennonite Boarding School)
Dwight Mission School—Marble City/Vian
El Meta Bond College
Emahaka Academy
Euchee Boarding School (Yuchi)
Eufaula Boarding School (Eufala Dormitory)
Folsom Training School (Willis Folsom Institute)
Fort Coffee Academy
Fort Sill Indian School
Galloway College (Willie Halsell College)
Haloche Indian Mission School (The Industrial Institute for the Deaf, Blind, and Orphans of the Colored Race)
Harrell International Institute (Spaulding Female College)
Hillside Mission School (Skiatook Friends' School)
International School of Blind and Deaf
Iowa Mission
Jones Male Academy
Kaw Boarding School
Koonaha Female Seminary
Lanubbee Female Seminary
Lone Wolf Boarding School
Mary Gregory Memorial Mission School
McCabe Boarding School (Pawhuska Boarding School)
Mekusukey Academy
Methvin Institute
Murray State School of Agriculture
Murrow Orphan Home (Murrow Indian Children's Home)
Nazareth Institute
New Hope Academy
Norwalk Academy for Boys
Nuyaka School and Orphanage
Oak Hill Industrial Academy (Elliot Academy)
Oak Ridge Manual Labor School
Oklahoma Presbyterian College for Girls (Calvin Institute; Durant Presbyterian College)
Old Goodland Indian Orphanage (Old Goodland Indian Orphanage Industrial School; Old Goodland Academy)
Oneida Boarding and Day School (Concho Indian Boarding School)
Osage Boarding School
Otoe Boarding School
Park Hill Mission School
Pawnee Boarding and Training School
Pecan Creek Mission School
Ponca Boarding School
Presbyterian for Indian Girls (Henry Kendall College; Minerva Home)
Quapaw Boarding School (Ottawa Industrial Boarding School)
Rainy Mountain Boarding School
Red Moon Boarding School
Riverside Indian School
Sacred Heart Institute

Sacred Heart Mission (St. Benedict's Industrial School; St. Mary's Industrial School)
Sasakwa Female Academy
Sac and Fox Indian Boarding School
Seger Indian Training School
Seneca Boarding School (Seneca, Shawnee, and Wyandotte Industrial Boarding School)
Sequoyah Orphan Training School (Sequoyah Indian High School)
Spencer Academy (Choctaw Academy)
St. Agnes Academy
St. Agnes Mission
St. Elizabeth's Boarding School
St. John's School for Osage Indian Boys
St. Joseph's Preparatory School
St. Joseph's School
St. Louis School for Osage Indian Girls
St. Mary's Mission School
St. Patrick's Mission and Boarding School (Anadarko Boarding School)
Tullahassee Boarding School
Tushka Lusa Institute
Tuskahoma Female Academy
Union Mission School
Wapanucka Institute (Allen Academy; Chickasaw Rock Academy)
Wealaka Boarding School
Wetumka Boarding School (Creek National Boarding School; Levering Manual Labor Boarding)
Wewoka Mission School (Ramsey Mission School)
Washita Boarding School
Wheelock Academy

OREGON (13)

Chemawa Indian Training School (Salem Indian School; Harrison Institute)
Forest Grove Indian Training School
Grand Ronde Boarding School
Indian Manual Labor Training School (Oregon Institute; Willamette University)
Kate Drexel Industrial Boarding School
Klamath Agency Boarding School
Mission Bottom Manual Labor Training School
Siletz Boarding School (Liberty Industrial School)
Simnasho Boarding and Day School
St. Andrew's Industrial Boarding (St. Ann's Mission)
Umatilla Boarding and Day School
Warm Springs Boarding and Day School
Yainax Indian Boarding School

PENNSYLVANIA (6)

Carlisle Indian Industrial School
Holy Providence School for Indians and Colored People
Lincoln Institution
Martinsburg School (Juniata Institute)
St. Francis Industrial School (St. Francis)
West Philadelphia Industrial School

SOUTH DAKOTA (35)

All Saint's School
Ascension Girls Boarding School
Brainard Indian Training School
Chamberlain Indian School
Cheyenne River Agency Boarding School
Cheyenne-Eagle Butte Boarding School
Crow Creek Agency Boarding School (Fort Thompson Indian School)
Crow Creek Tribal School
Fort Bennett Boarding School (Cheyenne River Agency Boarding School for Indian Boys)
Flandreau Indian School (Riggs Institute)
Good Will Mission Boarding School
Grace Mission Home Boarding and Day School (Grace Howard)
Grand River Boarding School
Hare Industrial School
Hope Indian Boarding School (Springfield Indian School)
Immaculate Conception Mission School (Stephan Mission School)
Lower Brule Industrial Boarding School
Oahe Boarding School (Peoria Flats Mission School)
Our Lady of Lourdes School
Pierre Indian School (Pierre Indian Learning Center)
Pine Ridge Boarding School (Oglala Indian Training School; Pine Ridge School)
Plum Creek Boarding School
Rapid City Indian School (Sioux San Hospital)
Red Cloud Indian School (Holy Rosary Mission)
Rosebud Agency Boarding and Day School
Sisseton Agency Boarding and Day School
St. Benedict Mission (Indian Farm School; Martin Kenel Boarding School)
St. Elizabeth's School
St. Francis Indian Mission School
St. John's School for Girls
St. Joseph's Indian School
St. Mary's School for Girls (Ascension Girls Boarding Schools)
St. Paul's Indian Mission School (Marty Indian School)
Tekakwitha Indian Mission and Orphanage
Yankton Industrial Boarding School

TENNESSEE (1)

Brainerd Mission School (Chickamauga Mission)

UTAH (7)

Aneth Boarding and Day School (Aneth Community School)
Intermountain Indian School
Navajo Faith Mission
Ouray Indian School (Uncompahgre Boarding School)
Panguitch Boarding School
St. George Southern Utah Boarding School (Shebit School)
Uintah Boarding and Day School (White Rocks Boarding School; Ute Indian Boarding School)

VERMONT (1)

Castleton Academy (Castleton University)

VIRGINIA (1)

Hampton Institute (Hampton University)

WASHINGTON (17)

Chehalis Boarding and Day School
Colville Mission School
Cushman Indian School
Fort Simcoe Indian Boarding School (Yakima Indian Boarding School)
Fort Spokane Boarding School
Neah Bay Boarding and Day School
Quinaielt Boarding and Day School
S'Kokomish Boarding and Day School
Sacred Heart Academy (Goodwin Mission School for Indians)
St. Francis Regis Mission School
St. George Indian Residential School
St. Joseph's Boarding School
St. Mary's Mission School (Pascal Sherman Indian School)
Stickney Home Mission School for Indians
Tonasket Boarding School (Okanagan Boarding School)
Tulalip Mission School (St. Anne's Catholic Mission; Tulalip Mission School of Our Lady of Seven Dolors)
Tulalip Indian Industrial School

WISCONSIN (14)

Bayfield Mission Boarding and Day School (Holy Family Mission School)
Bethany Mission School—Ingersoll
Good Shepherd Industrial School (House of the Good Shepherd)
Hayward Boarding School
Lac du Flambeau Boarding School
Lutheran Mission School (Red Springs Boarding School)
Menominee Boarding School (Green Bay Boarding School; Keshena School; Menominee Tribal School)
Oneida Boarding and Day School
St. Mary's Catholic Indian Boarding School (Odanah)
St. Joseph Industrial School
Tomah Indian Industrial School
Winnebago Indian Mission—Black River Falls
Wittenberg Indian School (Bethany Indian Mission)
Zoar Mission Boarding School

WYOMING (6)

Arapaho Boarding and Day School
Shoshone Boarding and Day School
Shoshone-Episcopal Mission Boarding School (Robert's School)
St. Michael's Mission (The Church of Our Father's House)
St. Stephen's Mission Industrial School (St. Stephens Indian School)
Wind River Boarding School (Shoshone Agency Boarding School; Gravy High; Fort Washakie School District #21)

RESOURCES FOR YOUNG READERS

BOOKS

Indian Horse by Richard Wagamese
My Name Is Seepeetza by Shirley Sterling
No Time to Say Goodbye: Children's Stories of Kuper Island Residential School by Sylvia Olsen
Stealing Little Moon by Dan SaSuWeh Jones
They Called It Prairie Light: The Story of Chilocco Indian School by K. Tsianina Lomawaima

MUSEUMS

Heard Museum in Phoenix, Arizona
Stewart Indian School Cultural Center & Museum in Carson City, Nevada
Genoa U.S. Indian School Foundation Museum in Genoa, Nebraska
National Museum of the American Indian in Washington, D.C.

BIBLIOGRAPHY

Adams, David Wallace. *Education for Extinction: American Indians and the Boarding School Experience, 1875–1928*. University Press of Kansas, 1995.

Bloom, John. *To Show What an Indian Can Do: Sports at Native American Boarding Schools*. University of Minnesota Press, 2000.

Carlisle Indian School Digital Resource Center. https://carlisleindian.dickinson.edu/.

Child, Brenda J. *Boarding School Seasons: American Indian Families, 1900–1940*. University of Nebraska Press, 1998.

Child, Brenda J. "Runaway Boys, Resistant Girls: Rebellion at Flandreau and Haskell, 1900–1940." *Journal of American Indian Education* 35, no. 3 (Spring 1996): 49–57.

DeLuca, Richard. " 'We Hold the Rock!': The Indian Attempt to Reclaim Alcatraz Island." *California History* 62, no. 1 (Spring 1983): 2–22.

Dunbar-Ortiz, Roxanne. *An Indigenous Peoples' History of the United States*. Beacon Press, 2014.

Fear-Segal, Jacqueline, and Susan D. Rose, eds. *Carlisle Indian Industrial School: Indigenous Histories, Memories, and Reclamations*. University of Nebraska Press, 2016.

Fortunate Eagle, Adam. *Pipestone: My Life in an Indian Boarding School*. University of Oklahoma Press, 2010.

Gross, Lawrence W. "Humor and Healing in the Nonfiction Works of Jim Northrup." *Wicazo Sa Review* 24, no. 1 (Spring 2009): 65–87.

Hoefel, Roseanne. "Walking with Jim Northrup and Sharing His 'Rez'ervations." *Studies in American Indian Literatures* 9, no. 2 (Summer 1997): 11–21.

Jacobs, Margaret D. *White Mother to a Dark Race: Settler Colonialism, Maternalism, and the Removal of Indigenous Children in the American West and Australia, 1880–1940*. University of Nebraska Press, 2009.

Johnson, David L., and Raymond Wilson. "Gertrude Simmons Bonnin, 1876–1938: 'Americanize the First American.' " *American Indian Quarterly* 12, no. 1 (Winter 1988): 27–40.

Johnson, Troy R. "The State and the American Indian: Who Gets the Indian Child?" *Wicazo Sa Review* 14, no. 1 (Spring 1999): 197–214.

Kotlowski, Dean J. "Alcatraz, Wounded Knee, and Beyond: The Nixon and Ford Administrations Respond to Native American Protest." *Pacific Historical Review* 72, no. 2 (May 2003): 201–27.

Langston, Donna Hightower. "American Indian Women's Activism in the 1960s and 1970s." *Hypatia* 18, no. 2 (Spring 2003): 114–32.

Leahy, Todd, and Nathan Wilson, eds. "My First Days at the Carlisle Indian School by Howard Gansworth: An Annotated Manuscript." *Pennsylvania History: A Journal of Mid-Atlantic Studies* 71, no. 4 (Autumn 2004): 479–93.

Lewandowski, Tadeusz. *Red Bird, Red Power: The Life and Legacy of Zitkala-Ša.* University of Oklahoma Press, 2016.

Lomawaima, K. Tsianina. *They Called It Prairie Light: The Story of Chilocco Indian School.* University of Nebraska Press, 1994.

Maraniss, David. *Path Lit by Lightning: The Life of Jim Thorpe.* Simon & Schuster, 2022.

Martínez, David. "A City upon Stolen Land: Westward Expansion, Indigenous Intellectuals, and the Origin of Resistance." *Journal of the Early Republic* 43, no. 4 (Winter 2023): 607–17.

Middleton, Richard. "Pontiac: Local Warrior or Pan-Indian Leader?" *Michigan Historical Review* 32, no. 2 (Fall 2006): 1–32.

National Native American Boarding School Healing Coalition. "Indian Boarding Schools in the United States." National Native American Boarding School Healing Coalition, 2024.

Ostler, Jeffrey. *Surviving Genocide: Native Nations and the United States from the American Revolution to Bleeding Kansas.* Yale University Press, 2019.

Parks, Keiteyana I. "Indigenous Boarding Schools in the United States and Canada: Potential Issues and Opportunities for Redress as the United States Government Initiates Formal Investigation." *American Indian Law Review* 47, no. 1 (2022–23): 37–70.

Rosenfelt, Daniel M. "Indian Schools and Community Control." *Stanford Law Review* 25, no. 4 (April 1973): 489–550.

Rosier, Paul C. "The Association on American Indian Affairs and the Struggle for Native American Rights, 1948–1955." *The Princeton University Library Chronicle* 67, no. 2 (Winter 2006): 366–91.

Sakiestewa Gilbert, Matthew T. " 'The Hopi Followers': Chief Tawaquaptewa and Hopi Student Advancement at Sherman Institute, 1906–1909." *Journal of American Indian Education* 44, no. 2 (2005): 1–23.

Sheinkin, Steve. *Undefeated: Jim Thorpe and the Carlisle Indian School Football Team.* Roaring Brook Press, 2017.

White Hawk, Sandy. "Excerpt from 'A Child of the Indian Race': A Story of Return." *Minnesota History* 68, no. 4 (Winter 2022–23): 144–49.

Woolford, Andrew. *This Benevolent Experiment: Indigenous Boarding Schools, Genocide, and Redress in Canada and the United States.* University of Nebraska Press, 2015.

Zitkála-Šá. *American Indian Stories, Legends, and Other Writings.* Edited by Cathy N. Davidson and Ada Norris. Penguin Classics, 2003.

Zitkála-Šá. "The School Days of an Indian Girl." *The Atlantic Monthly* 85 (1900): 185–194.

IMAGE CREDITS

Carlisle Indian School Digital Resource Center (xvii left, xvii right, 89, 112). Cumberland County Historical Society, Carlisle, PA (87, 101). Gale Family Library, Minnesota Historical Society (100, 104, 128). Illinois Department of Natural Resources (15). Library of Congress (74, 79). National Archives (11, 143). National Museum of the American Indian, Smithsonian Institution (107, 161, 170). National Park Service (163). Public Domain (28). South Dakota State Historical Society (92).